To
Terry
Enjoy the book

Jack

THE JOURNEY

HUNTING THE WORLD

A LIFE OF DREAMS

JOHN McATEER

PUBLISHED BY FIDELI PUBLISHING, INC.

ISBN: 978-1-948638-64-7

Published by

Fideli Publishing, Inc.
119 W. Morgan St.
Martinsville, IN 46151

www.FideliPublishing.com

This book is lovingly dedicated to my family.

Acknowledgements

A heartfelt thank you to Bob Foulkrod, who has been a true inspiration by making me push harder to achieve my goals.

To Bear Magnet executive producer Dale Boyer for having the trust and faith in my ability to serve in an industry that I truly love: the outdoors.

To all the outfitters and guides who work so hard to make the outdoors such a great adventure, making all our dreams come true I thank You.

Most of all, to the men and women who are unable to hunt and long for the outdoors, may they be able to live their dreams through the journals and passages of the writers who have had these great adventures.

TABLE OF CONTENTS

ENDORSEMENTS

My Long Time Friend has put his Dreams and Goals into a Book ' whether you are working on your First Dream hunt or veteran Hunter that's been on many dream hunts 'this is a must read. As you read along I'm sure it will help plan on making your own memories or the many adventures you have already been on . Enjoy!

Bob Foulkrod

ENDORSEMENTS (CONTINUED)

Legendary John McAteer, the gentle giant, the educator, the professional hunter, the family man, and one of, if not the hardest working man on this planet. There's not much else that describes this amazing man other than he's a long-time dear friend, and the angel/devil of wisdom on my shoulders. John has been my Director of Operations for the past four years, although hinting to retire, I won't allow it.... LOL.

When John McAteer speaks, he speaks from the heart with much added knowledge and experiences thrown in. John would help anyone in need... if you needed a shirt, he'd go without... if you needed food, John would give you his last penny. This is John McAteer.

John McAteer's many wilderness adventures have taken him around the globe, and I've only had the pleasure of listening to a few of his amazing stories. Now with this book, I'll be able to enjoy every story as if I was there along side him.

I personally thank John for all his contributions to the outdoor industry, he is a true conservationist.

Sincerely,

Dale G. Boyer
CEO BadBear Productions & Marketing Inc.

ENDORSEMENTS (CONTINUED)

This is a great read. John has experienced adventures all over the world and he has a unique storytelling talent in bridging the past to the present and makes you feel like you're right there with him. Congratulations and best wishes of success for this book. I recommend this to any outdoorsman who wants to immerse himself in an outdoor adventure.

Gus Congemi
Live The Wild Life, Pursuit Channel

INTRODUCTION

My hunting journey began in the autumn of 1963, when the air was crisp and the temperature was dropping. I was 14 and my family and I lived in a 12-story apartment complex in the Bronx. That place swarmed with children of all ages — a lot like living in a beehive — and was the exact opposite of living in the great untamed outdoors.

I remember the Monday that changed my life like it was yesterday. My father, a hard-working Irishman, came home from work, and as usual, stopped at the mailbox to collect that day's mail. He came inside and placed the mail on the hall table for my mother to sort, just as I happened to be passing by on my way outside. I looked down, and there it was, my future in the form of an *Outdoor Life* magazine.

I grabbed it and immediately went outside and sat down on the front step of our apartment building to devour everything inside. I was drawn into another world when I looked at those pages, and read each article like I'd found the source of all knowledge. I didn't want to miss a thing. I'd always liked the outdoors, but for some reason on that day like became love.

I can still recall that tingling feeling I got each time *Outdoor Life* arrived in our mailbox. This was my complete source for information on everything from outdoor equipment to clothing, and most important to me, hunting. Each month, I traveled the world through the magazine's photographs and words. When I was done reading, I felt like I'd climbed every mountain, crossed every river, and fished in every lake.

Because of all the reading I'd done, I thought I knew everything the outdoors could throw at me by the time I was 16. So, I saved the money I earned from my paper route and my weekend job at the local pet store and invested in a backpack and some simple hunting gear. At this point, nature and everything it encompassed had become my passion. I even joined the Boy Scouts so I could go camping and learn more about the great outdoors.

By the time I turned 18, I was ready to go experience things on my own. The only thing standing in my way was this major obstacle called the Vietnam War — Uncle Sam wanted me. So, I put my dreams on hold for a while and joined the United States Navy. I ended up serving on the USS *Bronson,* a naval destroyer.

✦　✦　✦

After I was discharged, I went to work in a bank. Like all my friends, I fell in love, married and had children. I had a full life, but it felt like something was missing.

My dream of exploring the outdoors rekindled itself with the first change in the weather in September of 1970. I decided that the time was right to pursue my lust for the hunt. So, in October of that year, I purchased my first hunting license, and planned my first deer hunt with fellow hunting enthusiasts I'd kept in touch with during my stint in the service.

These guys were also from the Bronx, so it was easy for us to plan various outings. We even started Mulers Hunting Club, because, like mules, we wanted to carry all our gear and equipment in our backpacks when we hunted.

They say each great adventure starts with that first step. My step into the outdoor life was when I decided to hunt white-tailed deer in the Catskill Mountains of New York with a few of my close friends from the Mulers Club.

This initial foray into the world of hunting in November of 1970 sparked an interest in harvesting game that would never wane. I was eventually inspired to travel from the Catskill Mountains in New York to high-altitude Tibetean peaks to the dark continent of Africa and across the Canadian provinces in pursuit various prey. My childhood dreams became reality, and I would travel the world doing what I loved.

Every little detail in those initial outings was a challenge for me. But, I never waivered in my quest for the hunt because I always felt the outdoors would take me to good places and show me great things. Failure was never really a consideration when I planned my hunts, but when I did inevitably fail, I used the knowledge I gained as a stepping-stone to propel my success.

I've learned through the years that you should always pursue your dreams, and never let them be tarnished by others. I constantly push myself to conquer whatever life throws at me. I've faced myriad obstacles in my life, but almost always overcame them. My reward for overcoming was being able to spend more time in the great outdoors.

Remember, nothing is more rewarding than living out your dreams.

MY FIRST HUNT: WHITE-TAILED DEER

Learning about and studying the magnificent white-tailed deer took my knowledge of hunting to a new level. I had to learn how to recognize my quarry's feeding patterns and figure out the effect the wind and moon cycles had on the hunt.

Back in the early days, not many products were available to assist the hunter in his efforts to hide his scent from quarry. Thus, the first few years of my hunting career were relatively unproductive. I made mistakes, but I vowed to learn from them and become a better hunter.

As I studied the white-tailed deer, I found myself trying to think like one. If I was the deer, where would I forage for food? Where would I find water? Eventually, I started thinking like a deer and that helped me find success.

I also learned how to read a topographical map so it would be easier for me to locate food sources and watering holes in the area where I'd be hunting. I also learned to study the wind when I got to my location. Once I knew the prevailing wind, I could figure out a pattern and select an area for my tree stand or natural ground blind.

For this particular excursion, the perfect position for the tree stand platform was 17 feet above the ground. This was high enough to keep my scent off the forest floor so the deer wouldn't smell me. I also built a second stand between feeding and bedding areas, as a back up if the wind shifted.

Where you choose to put your tree stand can be the determining factor for whether you harvest a deer or go home empty handed. I personally try to choose a covered spot, overlooking a well-worn trail that deer travel frequently. I choose trees that are strong and healthy enough to hold the tree stand and high enough so I don't have to worry about the deer getting a whiff of my scent.

✦ ✦ ✦

For tree stand positioning, I personally try to choose a covered spot, overlooking a well-worn trail that deer travel frequently. I choose trees that are strong and healthy enough to hold the tree stand and high enough so I don't have to worry about the deer getting a whiff of my scent.

My first hunt started on a crisp, clear October morning in 1970. I ventured out of my tent to greet the darkness with a hunger for the hunt. A small breeze was blowing in from the west as I set out, so I'd decided to put everything I'd learned to the test and outwit the great white-tailed deer.

Frost covered the grass that morning, and a hush hung in the air. The oak leaves whispered as they fell to the forest floor and at first light the forest suddenly came alive with all of God's tiny creatures starting their day. All at once, a heavier sound replaced the rustling of small animals, and I tried to figure out where it was coming from.

I decided to check out the area I'd seen when setting up my deer stand, hoping this would be where my scouting and planning would pay off. I was pretty sure one of the deer had been feeding all night and was returning to the bedding area I'd found.

I quickly climbed into the stand and looked in that direction. It wasn't long before the crunching of the the leaves heralded the arrival of my white-tailed deer. This was just like a scenario I'd read about in *Outdoor Life* all those years ago. The only difference was, this time I was experiencing it firsthand.

As the white-tailed deer approached, I paid strict attention to every move it made. As it got closer, I could see it was a doe. I was hunting for a buck, but was thankful I'd had the foresight to secure a doe permit, too.

I watched as her ears twitched with the wind. She was trying to pick up sounds of danger. My stand was set perfectly, so there was no way she could hear me or pick up my scent. As she approached, her ears suddenly pinned back and she turned her head. When she looked behind her, I knew another deer had to be following her.

I reached for my bow, analyzing the doe's every move. Low and behold, a few seconds later there was a beautiful eight-point buck coming down the trail behind her!

All my senses were heightened as I tried to put my years of reading and knowledge to work to create a successful

Eight-point Whietail buck, harvested in October in New York.

hunt. I didn't want to alert the animals to my presence so my movements were minimal.

As the buck wandered into the clearing, I drew my bow. I estimated him to be 20 yards in front of me, and he was exhibiting a broadside posture — a great setup for my shot.

I focused on his vital area and released my arrow. As I watched it fly, I realized it was dead-on. I finally had my first trophy! For me, the trophy wasn't about the size of his rack, it was about the memory of the hunt this great animal had given me.

Always remember that no matter what your quarry is, respect it, for it has fulfilled your dreams.

Venison Loaf

1-1/2 lb. shoulder of
   venison
3 or 4 slices of day-old
   bread made into 1-1/3
   cups loosely packed
   bread crumbs
3 tablespoons of finely
   chopped celery
3 tablespoons butter

1 cup water
1 medium bay leaf
Marrow
1-1/4 teaspoons salt
1/4 to 1/2 teaspoon
   marjoram (optional)
1-1/2 teaspoons grated
   onion
1 egg, slightly beaten

Wipe meat with a clean, damp cloth and trim off any tough tissue or strong-smelling fat. Remove bones and grind meat. There should be 1 lb. of ground meat when you're done. Save marrow.

Tear the slices of bread into small crumbs or pulse in food processor. Sauté celery in butter for 5 minutes; add water, bay leaf and simmer 3 minutes. Discard bay leaf. Combine cooled liquid with crumbs; add meat, marrow and remaining ingredients. Mix thoroughly.

Turn into a greased loaf pan (3-3/4 x 7-1/2 inches) and bake in a moderate oven (350° F) for 1 hour.

Serves 6.

Barbequed Venison Tenderloin

1 deer tenderloin (1-1/4 lb.)

2 tablespoons butter or shortening

Barbeque sauce:
1 cup catchup
2 tablespoons grated onion
1/2 cup chopped celery
1/2 cup water
2 teaspoons vinegar

1-1/2 teaspoons salt
1/4 to 1/2 teaspoon Worcestershire, as desired
Kick it up a bit by adding jalapeños or tabasco sauce to taste

Cut tenderloin into slices 1-3/4-inch thick (makes about 6). Trim off any strong fat or tough membrane.

Heat butter in a skillet and brown slices of deer quickly.

Meanwhile, combine remaining ingredients and pour over hot meat. Place uncovered in a moderate oven (350° F) for 1 hour.

Baste meat occassionally with the barbecue sauce and trun once during baking time.

Serves 6.

STALKING THE QUÉBEC BLACK BEAR

Black bears are unbelievably versatile animals that are fond of establishing habits. I call them creatures of convenience because they'll feast on anything from a decayed carcass to fresh fish to lush berries in the summertime.

I've seen black bears run just from sighting or smelling a human entering their domain, but I've also seen them charge an intruder while snapping their jaws. They are not animals to be taken lightly — black bears are responsible for most of the bear attacks in North America.

Because of the animals' fondness for repetitive behavior, hunting them is best achieved by using baited sites they can return to repeatedly. Choosing a site takes some research, since you want to locate it in an area bears frequent.

Once the site is selected, 55-gallon drums are filled with tasty treats and secured to trees. This will lure the bears to the site. This technique is the most popular way to harvest a worthy bear. Modern technology also allows for employing game cameras to monitor the site's activity to help time the date of the hunt.

✦　✦　✦

To find the Black Bear, I traveled to Québec during the first week of June. On the way to the site, I stopped and did the tourist thing — taking a picture of a dazzling waterfall. The blood-sucking Canadian insect population made sure I didn't look at the scenery for long. I knew that dealing with insects and their bites was the price I'd have to pay to hunt in prime season.

When bear hunting, hiring a guide through a reputable outfitter is essential. Outfitters, an individual or company, provide supplies, equipment, and guides to hunters. In this case I was happy to see that the guide who worked for the outfitter I'd hired had done his homework. Before I arrived, he had already blazed the trail and set up the bait barrels in a spot black bears frequented.

He offered them a seven-course meal, including pastries, bacon fat, gummy bears, blueberry syrup, popcorn, and other tasty, fragrant treats. Once the bears established a feeding pattern at the barrels, the guide watched to establish their habits. This allowed him to place the tree stands or blinds in the best positions according to wind patterns and how the bear would be hunted — bow or rifle.

Once the bears establishes a feeding pattern, you will know where to place the tree stands, according to what the wind is doing.

I prefer a ground blind to a tree stand. These can be either a camouflaged tent with windows or natural camouflage created with trees and brush, leaving a space big enough for a hunter to hide inside. I usually set my ground blind within 20 yards of the baited area, again depending upon wind direction. The trick to hunting in a ground blind is to make yourself comfortable because you might be in for a long wait.

I like this method bettter because I feel it puts me on the same level as the bear. I know of no greater excitement

Natural ground blind.

than being at eye level with a 300-pound bear. Watching him walk around me, not knowing what could happen at any given moment, is a thrill like no other.

It's amazing how I become so much more aware of everything around me when I'm hunting. In this case, I heard the small noises of a bear heading toward the #3 bait barrel. My heightened senses made the experience that much more intense.

Black bear hunting has different timing from everything else in the hunting realm. It's usually done from late afternoon to early evening, when bears are more active. This is their favorite time of day because the temperature cools down and there are fewer insects to deal with.

I chose a crossbow for this hunt, so I set up a range to sight in my bow to make sure I could ethically harvest my animal. (No hunter wants an animal to needlessly suffer.) I sighted the crossbow in at 20-30 yards, and it was on the money. I was using Black Eagle bolts, Grim Reaper broadheads, and Lumina knocks.

We got to the area where the bears had been sighted, and my guide and I re-baited the barrels with some fresh baked goods and bacon grease. While we were there, we checked the game cameras and saw three different bears frequenting the area, so we knew we were in a good spot. It was time to get into the ground blind and start waiting as we fended off the mosquitoes and black flies.

This time out was unproductive. It rained most of the night. At least the ground blind was nice and dry.

The guide and I decided to head back to camp as darkness set in and we were back and looking forward to a hot dinner by 10 p.m. We enjoyed our dinner as the rain danced off the tin roof of the cabin. Something about the rain hitting a metal roof always ensures I'll have a great night's sleep.

I awoke at first light, and by 8 a.m. my guide and I had devoured our breakfasts and were heading out in the boats. Our plans for the day included lake trout fishing before heading to the blind in the early evening. By 11 a.m. we had caught five trout, just the right number for an excellent meal.

We put our fish in the refrigerator back at camp, ate a quick lunch, and then headed to the blind. After the rain the day before, the mosquitoes and black flies were insane. Once we got inside the blind, however, I fired up my butane thermal cell to repel them. It works by heating up a coated pad that keeps insects from approaching. Thankfully, it provided instant relief!

At 4:30, I caught movement out off the corner of my eye. I turned and saw a bear approaching baited area #1 from behind the bait barrel. I was ready for him. I slipped my finger onto the safety and released my arrow.

Alas, the bear heard the click as it released, and that was all she wrote. He turned tail and skedaddled. That was it for activity that night.

The next day, with the sun high in the sky, my guide and I elected to hunt a different area five miles into the middle of nowhere. The bait site there looked good, and again I bequeathed more blood to the Canadian insects than I care to admit.

I had a terrific feeling about this site. The wind had shifted and was blowing in such a way that the bear wouldn't smell our presence. Before I knew it, an hour had passed and my first bear came into sight. First one cub, then another made an appearance, and finally mama waddled up behind them.

I watched them for two hours, which was a lot of fun. The cubs chased a pine marten around the bait barrel until they wore themselves out. Eventually, they ambled off into the dense forest with their mother. After they'd left, we called it a night and trudged back to camp, a bit defeated.

The next day we hoped our luck would change, and headed back to the original bait site. I hoped that first bear I'd seen had come back overnight. We checked the game camera, and lo and behold, he had indeed come back. I settled in for the night and watched red squirrels climb in and

Nearly 200 pound Black Bear harvested in Rumford, Maine.

out of the bait barrel, stealing treats and running like hell up the nearest tree.

The sky turned cloudy at 8:15, and a short time later a bear visited. It wasn't the same bear I'd seen the first night, but he seemed committed. This time, I got truly ready. As he approached, I waited for him to present a broadside shot. When he did, I knocked the arrow in my Lumina knock, which lights up to show the flight of the arrow, and squeezed the trigger on my crossbow. It let go and my Black Eagle arrow flew on a beautiful trajectory.

My shot pierced both of the bear's lungs. He ran off, but didn't get far. I called my guide and told him I'd harvested a bear, then stayed in the blind until the guide got there. We then we searched the thick, dark forest to retrieve my kill.

I would guess this bear had a live weight of approximately 200 pounds. He wasn't a monstrous size, but he was still a great harvest for me. We took the bear to the truck and headed back to the lodge.

I was elated that I'd shot a bear, and I was excited that I was going to have a delicious lake trout meal to culminate a super day.

The next morning, I capped out the bear, removing and salting the hide and preserving the meat for transportation. When we got back to civilization, I unrolled the hide and stored it in the walk-in cooler at the outfitter's main lodge.

I would recommend bear hunting to all sportsmen and sportswomen. It's thrilling and unpredictable and, like many other hunting endeavors, rewarding.

Bear Loin Steaks

2 loin steaks, 2-1/2 lbs., 5/8
    to 3/4-inch thick*
1 tablespoon butter or
    margerine, melted

2 teaspoons lemon juice
1-1/4 teaspoons salt
Generous dash of pepper
1/2 cup boiling water

Wipe steaks clean with a damp cloth. Trim off all the fat because it has a strong flavor. This should leave about 1-1/2 lbs. lean steak.

Place steak on a hot, greased broiler rack set 4 inches from heat. Combine butter and lemon juice and brush over top of steaks. Sprinkle with half of the salt and pepper. Broil 7 to 8 minutes.

Turn steaks, brush with remaining lemon-butter and remaining salt and pepper. Broil another 7 or 8 minutes for well-done steaks.

Remove from broiler to platter. Drizzle 1/2 cup water over rack and scrape down the residue into the drip pan. Remove rack. Stir gravy until well blended, reheat to boiling. Pour over hot steaks and serve immediately.

Serves 4 to 5.

*If the steaks seem tough, the meat may be pounded or diced as in preparation for cubed steak.

Bear Stew

4 pounds bear meat, cubed
1/4 cup all-purpose flour
1 teaspoon dried oregano
1 teaspoon salt
1 teaspoon ground black
    pepper
4 tablespoons butter or
    margarine
2 tablespoons olive oil

1 onion, chopped
1 cup beef broth
4 bay leaves
2 pounds red potatoes,
    diced
1 pound fresh mushrooms
5 carrots, sliced
2 turnips, cubed

In a large mixing bowl combine flour, oregano, salt and pepper. Place bear meat in the bowl a little at a time and coat well.

Heat oil and butter in a large skillet. Fry the bear meat until browned. Let drain on paper towels.

Fill a large Dutch oven with 2 to 3 quarts water. Add bear meat, onions, beef broth, bay leaves, potatoes, mushrooms carrots and turnips.

Cook on medium-high heat for 2 to 3 hours. Add more water as needed.

WYOMING ANTELOPE HUNT

My passion for archery started when I was a young man. My idol growing up, and the person about whom I read in all of my outdoor magazines, was a true pioneer by the name of Fred Bear. I read every story I could find about his travels and hunting adventures. (Little did I know that someday he would present me with an award for one of my archery hunts.)

I wanted to bow hunt an antelope in the worst way. Wyoming has an excellent antelope population, and a good friend of mine, Jerry Matthews, just happens to live there. So, I decided to visit him and have a hunt. This wouldn't be my first time going after antelope, but I was looking forward to harvesting an animal that would qualify for Pope & Young Club's standards.

The Pope & Young criteria includes things like length of horn, circumference of base, circumference at first, send and third quarter and length of prong for each horn. Measurements must be done by an official measurer of the club. Using the measurement information, a final score is determined and that number creates becomes the animal's score. The higher scores are entered into their record books.

✦   ✦   ✦

Antelope hunting is extremely rewarding for both the novice and experienced sportsman. The challenges this animal presents make the hunt that much more exciting.

When hunting antelope with a bow and arrow, one usually hunts over a watering hole. This can become hot and boring at times for the hunter, since an average antelope only drinks once or twice a day.

Antelope are normally hunted on the open plains. This presents a problem for the hunter, because the endless array of undulating hills and valleys provide nothing to hide in or behind.

When hunting antelope with a bow and arrow, one usually hunts over a watering hole, which may be hot and boring at times. An average antelope may only go to a watering hole once or twice a day.

So, on this hunt Jerry and I built a hay bale blind. A hay bail blind is constructed of bails of hay and made by piling them on top of and around each other to create a small structure. They are normally set up to accommodate a 20 to 40 yard shot.  We left slot openings or "shooting ports" facing the water hole in this blind. We also installed a burlap roof to keep the sun off us and reduce the temperature inside.

Once I got settled in the blind, I took out my rangefinder and ranged the different aspects of the watering hole from front to back and side to side. I wanted to measure the distance between myself and where I expected the quarry to show up to help me know when to take the shot.

After using my rangefinder, I was certain this would be a successful hunt. The good news was the front edge of the watering hole was approximately 23 yards away. The bad news was the far side of the watering hole was 62 yards away, which was a distance a bit out of my wheelhouse.

Next, I checked my equipment. Whenever I go hunting, no matter what time I arrive at my destination, I never fail to do this check to make sure all of my equipment is in good working order.

I was using a Hoyt compound bow with Muzzy Broadhead graphite arrows this time around. After checking my bow and making a few adjustments, it was shooting precisely as I wanted it to.

At 5 a.m., the thermometer read 75 degrees in the blind. I settled in, checked out my field of view, and prepared for a long, hot day. I had my mystery lunch bag with me — you never knew what would be packed for you back the lodge — and I had plenty of water, which was good since I knew I'd probably be in for a long wait.

By noon, it was 87 degrees, and by 2 p.m. the temperature hit the 90 degree mark. Thank goodness for the burlap roof! By 5 p.m., the only animals I'd seen were prairie birds, so I called it a day.

Hot and a little discouraged, I drove back to Jerry's house and settled in for a quiet evening. I had an exquisite dinner of elk backstraps wrapped in bacon, grilled potatoes, fresh broccoli, and a cold beer, then went to bed with my mind busily planning what I'd do to make my hunt successful the next day.

By 5 a.m. the next morning, I was back in my burlap covered condo. One of the greatest things for me about being a sportsman is settling in the woods, on the plains, or in the mountains before morning light, because you get to hear and see nature waking up.

As dawn broke, I noticed a few female antelope stepping into the water. They were cautious and seemed unsure of the area. The problem was, they'd arrived on the far side of the watering hole, which was too far away from my position for my bow to be effective.

I watched every move they made as they scanned the area for danger. Their body language told a valuable story. After finishing a long drink of water, they moved off into the meadow.

By that time, my day had come to an end. It was just too hot in the blind. I'd spent several hours sweating and hoping, but the buck I'd been dreaming of never made an appearance.

I trudged back to the truck, and headed to the house, an hour away. After supper, I went to bed, setting my alarm clock to go off extra early. I was determined to make the next day a success.

✦ ✦ ✦

The next morning, I quickly drank two big cups of coffee and jumped into the truck by 4 a.m. I was excited because I'd decided to try the other area I'd set up.

I walked three-quarters of a mile to get to the blind, and then ranged the watering hole nearest me. The close side turn out to be 20 yards away, with the far side measured 40.

At 10 a.m., two majestic mule deer headed for the watering hole. I loved watching them. They'd had their fill of water and left the area by 11:30.

By then, the temperature had reached 96 degrees. I was sweltering in my blind. I suddenly saw movement out of the corner of my eye. I glanced to the right side of the watering hole and saw two antelope heading my way.

Twenty-five minutes later, they were at the watering hole and I was set up and ready. The first two were young, but then a big boy arrived. It seemed like it took him forever to commit to drinking some water.

Finally, he relaxed and took a long drink, leaving me an exceptional broadside shot. I shot him straight through his lungs at 40 yards with a graphite arrow. He ran thirty yards and then piled up.

The day was so hot that Jerry, my guide, had remained at camp, so I radioed him about my kill, and he appeared 20 minutes later to help retrieve my antelope.

Once again, nature had allowed me to make a great deposit in my memory bank. This buck was a fine representation of an antelope and quite a prize .

A fine representation of an antelope and quite a prize, harvested in Casper, Wyoming.

My friends often ask me what I do on vacation, and I tell them I sit in a tree or blind for a whole day in sometimes extreme weather. When they ask me why I want to do that, my answer is always, "I love it!"

Braised Antelope Chops in Mushroom Gravy

4 good-sized loin chops
   (weight about 1-1/2 lbs.)
1-3/4 teaspoons salt
Pinch of pepper
3 tablespoons butter
1 cup water

10-1/2 oz. can mushroom
   soup
1 teaspoon sherry
Tabasco or other hot sauce
   to tase

Wipe chops clean with a damp cloth and trim off any strong-smelling fat. Sprinkle chops with salt and pepper.

Use a skillet with tight-fitting cover to brown chops slowly (uncovered) on both sides in heated butter. Add 1/4 cup of water, cover and simmer 15 minutes, then add 1/4 cup more water and again cover and simmer 15 minutes.

Next, add the rest of the water and the soup. Cover and continue cooking very slowly for half an hour. Last, add sherry and Tobasco sauce. Serve at once.

Serves 4.

Antelope Goulash

1 tablespoon butter
1 pound ground antelope
    meat
1/4 cup chopped green bell
    pepper
1/4 cup chopped onion
2 tablespoons chopped
    fresh chives
1 (15.25 ounce) can whole
    kernel corn, drained
2 red potatoes, cubed

1 tomato, chopped
1 stalk celery, finely
    chopped
3 (14-ounce) cans beef
    broth
1 cup water
1 cup elbow macaroni
Salt and black pepper to
    taste
1/4 teaspoon garlic powder,
    or to taste

Stir butter, antelope, bell pepper, onion, and chives together in a large pot over medium heat until the vegetables are very tender and the antelope has browned, about 10 minutes.

Stir in the corn, red potatoes, celery, tomato, beef broth, water, and macaroni. Bring to a boil over high heat; reduce heat to medium-low, cover, and simmer until the potatoes are tender, about 30 minutes.

Season to taste with salt, pepper, and garlic powder before serving.

Sweet and Spicy Antelope with Mushrooms

Antelope backstrap sliced into 1/4-inch pieces
1/4 teaspoon garlic powder
1/4 teaspoon cumin
1/4 teaspoon turmeric
3-4 tablespoons butter
2 tablespoons mango chutney
1/4 cup sliced sweet onion
4 sliced Portobello mushrooms
1-2 diced Thai red and green chilis (the more the better, if you like spicy)
Fresh Thai basil or chives for garnish

Cut antelope backstrap into eight 1/2-inch thick pieces. In separate bowl, mix garlic powder, cumin and turmeric together and rub on both sides of the antelope pieces. Set meat aside.

Heat cast iron skillet on medium-high heat. Melt butter and add onion and mushrooms. Cook until onions become translucent, 5-8 minutes. Add chutney and Thai chilis and stir. Move to the side of the pan.

Add meat to the same pan and cook for 1-2 minutes, then turn and cook other side for 1 minute. (This will ensure that the antelope remains tender and flavorful.)

Stir antelope into mushrooms and onions. Remove to platter and garnish with fresh Thai basil or chives.

5-DAY HUNT FOR MOUNTAIN CARIBOU

My next quest sent me to British Columbia to work with a fantastic outfitter, Love Bros. & Lee. My first trip with them was a bow hunt for Stone Sheep, and it was phenomenal. I had one of the greatest guides, Bill Love, and looked forward to working with him again.

I had immense confidence in Bill's ability as a woodsman, and I knew Fred Bear, the most famous bow hunter at the time, wouldn't hunt the British Columbia region without Bill as his guide. Bill also worked with Fess Parker, TV's Daniel Boone. I knew he'd make sure I had a fantastic Mountain Caribou hunt.

✦ ✦ ✦

Bill met me at the airport and we drove to the floatplane base together. We loaded our gear into the plane and were soon airborne. Traveling to remote places like this by plane gives you a bird's eye view of the wilderness so you can see how truly beautiful Mother Nature is. As we flew over the mountaintops, we caught sight of some mountain goats and stone sheep to whet our hunter's appetites.

The floatplane landed on a remote lake. Cabins nestled into the hillside surrounded it. This would be our home base. The cabins were fabulously rustic and the scenery here was off the charts. My cabin sat on a hilltop overlooking the lake, and the view made my morning coffee taste even better.

Since we'd hunted together before, Bill knew my strengths and weakness, so we could move things along quickly. Bill, certainly didn't have many weaknesses. When I first met him, he'd just celebrated his 75th birthday and could out-walk men many years younger than him.

I brought my dependable Fred Bear Polar LTD bow along for this hunt. I checked it for accuracy before leaving, which is a habit I'll never break. Checking my bow makes me feel more confident that I'll harvest an animal in a quick and humane way.

My friends John and Joe joined me on this trip, and I enjoyed the walk with them as we meandered down to the lake to fish. After fishing, we drove along the shoreline of the lake. As I always say, the dirt never lies. The beach was covered in grizzly bear tracks. We also saw some cow moose and a few mountain goats up on the mountain.

My friend John had a mountain goat tag issued by the state, so I knew he was going to score on this trip. Joe had a tag for a moose, and I knew his guide would find what he was looking for.

After the morning fishing excursion, Bill and I went out and covered a lot of territory. I felt so privileged to be able to utilize his knowledge of the area. He's a living legend in the sporting industry, and that reputation is well deserved.

I loved hearing his stories as we trekked to our destination. He told several about Fred Bear and Fess Parker, and I enjoyed every minute.

We hunted for several hours, and by 3 p.m. we'd decided to make our way back to camp.

I was up early the next morning, and Bill and I hopped into the boat before my morning coffee had a chance to settle in my stomach. We worked our way down the lake to an abandoned trappers' shack. We left the boat there, then climbed up the mountain so we could glass.

Standing high on that vantage point, I looked through my spotting scope to see where the animals were. On the way down, we hoped to find a nice bull caribou.

As the day progressed, we bumped into my friend John and his guide. They'd seen a large mountain goat in a difficult area, so they'd decide to stalk it until it moved to a better location. They'd worked their way up the mountain but realized they might lose the animal because they couldn't see it as they moved position.

I told John I'd help him with his goat rather than continuing my search for caribou. I offered to make my way back to the cabin on the opposite side of the lake so I'd be in front of the goat. I was wearing a red vest, so John could see me easily with his binoculars. I would move either my right or left arm to indicate how the goat had moved. If I raised my hand straight up, it would mean the goat was stationary.

Everything went smoothly. The guide and John reached the top of the mountain, and John climbed up higher to position himself above the mountain goat. He braced his rifle

on an outcropping of rock, took aim and fired, making the perfect shot. There was a problem, though. When he hit the goat, it rolled off the mountain and fell about 800 feet.

I saw John and the guide crawling down the side of the mountain, trying to find that goat. I couldn't see it from where I was, so I decided to wait at the cabin until John returned that evening ... with his goat. It was a beautiful Billy with a great set of horns that measured about eight inches. John had now officially filled his tag. I congratulated him on a job well done.

Bill and I covered a lot of territory the next day. We climbed to the upper valleys to glass down below, but we couldn't find a mountain caribou. We looked until it started to get dark, then headed back to the boat and motored to camp.

We got back at dusk and gobbled up a five-star meal, which consisted of roast turkey, stuffing, mashed potatoes, fresh broccoli, and sweet potato pie. It doesn't get any better than that!

The camp consisted of four cabins located on a pristine lake, with three cabins for designated for hunters and the remaining cabin acting as the mess hall. The cook employed there was second to none.

Going into day three of the five-day hunt, I wasn't too concerned about the caribou. There is no guarantee on any hunting trip, so with that in mind, we loaded up the boat and off we went. All was in readiness, and the only thing I had to do was find the caribou.

We saw a beautiful moose on the shoreline that day. I wish I could've told Joe about it, since it would've been a great one for him to harvest. Another highlight of this trip was that I saw a beautiful, mature lynx. You never know what you're going to see when you're wandering the great outdoors.

Day three came and went. We hunted hard, we walked a lot, and we didn't see a single caribou.

The next day, my alarm clock sounded off at 4:30 a.m. and by 6:10 we bounded into the boat and set off once again. When we landed at a new location, we climbed up to an outcropping of rock so that I could glass a valley.

Bill tapped me on the shoulder and told me he'd seen a caribou enter the lake. He thought it was likely going to swim to the other side. We hurried down the mountain to try to get an idea of where he was going.

Three-quarters of the way down, I saw the caribou step out of the lake and walk along the beachfront toward an abandoned trapper's shack.

I ran after him as fast as my legs could carry me. After hunting caribou on two previous trips, I knew I wanted to get ahead of him. If he stayed on his original path, I might be able to find a good ambush point somewhere down the line.

This one looked like a legal caribou, which meant he had ten points on one side. Since this was day four of this hunt and he was the only caribou I'd seen, I decided to take a shot.

The bull sauntered along the beachfront, 400 yards from where he'd exited the lake. I was 20 yards into the timber, making my shot at approximately 40 yards. Once again, I was using my Fred Bear Polar LTD bow. This bow had never let me down; it was always accurate.

In the time it took me to draw the bow back and lock it into position, the caribou caught sight of me. I let go of the arrow and hit him, and he ran into the timber. I was concerned about the shot because I'd sprinted down the mountain so fast that when I got into position I was breathing hard and a little shaky.

As I closed the distance, I could see my caribou on the edge of a sun-drenched shoreline. As in all my hunts, I

Mountain caribou harvested in British Columbia with outfitter Love Bros. & Lee.

skinned and quartered the animal and then loaded it into the boat and headed back to camp. I had my caribou, and I was a happy hunter.

We had a lot to talk about that night in camp. Between John's success with his mountain goat and me harvesting the mountain caribou, it made for great campfire conversation. Joe, unfortunately, had a tough time with his bull moose. He took a shot at one, but he didn't recover it.

I would recommend Love Bros. & Lee to any sportsman looking for a great hunt and a great adventure. Always remember that your memories are the footprint and the roadmap to your goals. When the day comes that you cannot hunt like you used to, your memories will enrich you as you sit in your easy chair, gazing at all of your trophies.

Caribou Stroganoff

1-1/2 lb. Caribou steak or
    boneless stewing meat
    (cut in 1/2 inch strips)
1/2 cup flour
1/2 teaspoon salt
1/2 lb mushrooms, chopped
1 large onion, chopped
1 clove garlic, minced
3 tablespoons Llard or

bacon fat
1 tablespoon Worcestershire
    sauce
1 beef bouillon cube
1 cup water
1 cup sour cream
steamed rice or noodles
paprika

Pound meat to tenderize if needed, though good quality steaks will not need this. (You can also use ground meat.)

Mix 1/4 cup flour with salt and dredge meat. In a large skillet, sauté garlic, onions and mushrooms in fat for 5 minutes. Remove them, add meat and brown. Remove meat from pan.

Dislove bullion cube in water. Add remaining flour to drippings in pan and stir. Add Worcestershire and the dissolved bouillon. Cook until thickened.

Add sour cream. Heat until gravy simmers, then add the meat and vegetables and heat. Serve over rice or noodles. Sprinkle with paprika to garnish.

Cherry Caribou Tenderloin

1 Caribou tenderloin
1 teaspoon salt
Pinch of pepper for
    seasoning
3 tablespoons butter
    (unsalted)

1/4 cup shallots, sliced
1/2 cup aged Balsamic
    vinegar
1/2 cup cherry preserves

Season tenderloin with salt and pepper. Melt butter in a skillet and sear meat on both sides until medium rare, then let it rest.

In a small skillet add 1 tablespoon butter and shallots. Sauté 3 minutes. Add pepper, salt, vinegar and cherry preserves and sauté until sauce slightly thickens. Add remaining butter to sauce and stir.

Slice tenderloin thin, arrange on serving dish and pour sauce over it.

NEWFOUNDLAND WOODLAND CARIBOU

When I returned from the Mountain Caribou hunt, I was glad to see my family and be home. After enjoying wonderful home-cooked meal, I sat by the fire and my mind turned to my next adventure. Since I'd achieved my dream of hunting Mountain Caribou, I decided to focus on the Woodland Caribou next. Constantly focusing on the next big adventure is what keeps me going. I've always said there's an end for every great beginning and when you reach that end, you get to start anew.

As always, I studied the habitat of my quarry, and concentrated on the Canadian province of Newfoundland this time. I had a good friend there who ran a caribou and moose camp. My interest was piqued and soon I was on the phone with my friend, making reservations.

✦　✦　✦

I spent the next two months planning. After researching my options, I selected an outfitter called TRI-T Camps. I decided to make some changes this time around, and would drive rather than fly to Newfoundland. I wanted to be able to bring home all of the caribou meat, if I got lucky enough to tag one.

I left on a cool day in late September, and traveled to Maine before getting on a ferry to Nova Scotia. I drove through Nova Scotia and boarded another ferry for an 11-hour cruise that would end at the island of Newfoundland.

The long ferry ride was pleasant. I boarded, then retired to a sleeping berth during the nighttime hours. I woke up in the morning feeling refreshed and alert. As we neared land, I got into my truck; I was almost at my destination.

My outfitter was waiting for me on the dock as I pulled my truck off. I followed him to the outfitter's house where he introduced me to his guiding staff. They packed my gear onto an Argo, an amphibious vehicle can travel on both land and water, and two four-wheelers.

That done, we set our sites on getting to camp, which was a six-hour trek. The Argo accommodated some of our gear, two hunters and a guide. The four-wheelers also carried gear and two more hunters, while towing a wagon filled with more supplies. (A few friends I'd been hunting with over the years had joined me for this hunt.)

The ride into camp was long and rough. My guide, a staff member, and I saw a lot of moose, and a bear as we traveled.

We arrived just as darkness set in. The best part of the day was what I heard after settling into my small rustic cabin — the dinner bell. The camp cook whipped up a fabulous meal for us, including homemade apple pie.

We all sat around the campfire, and like always, told stories about all of our great hunting trips and the people we'd met over the years. We decided to get a good night's sleep, and turned in early.

As morning broke over the pristine lake, I could hear the outboard motors already running on the boats. Everyone finished breakfast quickly and set out over the tundra.

We decided to sight in our rifles, to make sure they hadn't been jostled on the ride in. I had chosen a Winchester rifle in a 7mm caliber for this trip. Believe it or not, even though the trip in had been difficult, my rifle barely needed adjusted.

For the rest of the day we did some fantastic fishing, and I knew that my future would include a fabulous fresh trout dinner. After dinner, I sat and enjoyed nature and realized I was excited about the chance to explore the Canadian tundra. The morning couldn't come fast enough for me.

We departed in the dark the next morning. My guide, a great woodsman, and I traveled far and covered a lot of ground. I saw five Bull Moose , three cows and one heck of a monster black bear within the first hour — but no Caribou.

We got back to camp at dark, and everyone gathered around the dinner table to compare notes about our days. Then, we enjoyed a tasty dinner.

Afterward, came one of my favorite parts of each my hunting trips: hunter story hour. In this case, there were four hunters who each had amazing stories to tell.

One of my lifelong friends, Johnny B, was hunting for a moose on this trip. On the second day, while hunting with me, he got the opportunity to harvest a beautiful 50-inch moose (this is the antler measurement from the farthest point left to right). It was a real trophy by Newfoundland standards. My friend, Dave, who had a bear tag, also shot a 400-pound black bear that day.

The next morning, my guide and I made our way down to the boat and decided to go to the far end of the lake. We were still trying to find a nice bull Caribou. Once again, we saw moose and even saw some caribou, but they were all females. We couldn't seem to find a bull anywhere, even though we'd covered a lot of country.

Roy, a friend who also had a bull Caribou tag, was able to harvest a bull with exceptional mass to his horns. His was a great representation of Newfoundland Caribou.

Roy's guide skinned and capped the caribou for him, then quartered it and wrapped the quarters in cheesecloth to keep the flies off. When they got back to camp, that meat went into the meat house with the rest of the game bagged that week. When that was done, he put the Caribou horns on the roof of the meat house to dry.

The next morning, Roy's worst nightmare had come true. The horns were gone! A bear had visited the camp during the night and made off with Roy's trophy! This would've had even Daniel Boone and Davy Crockett in tears. Roy was devastated by the loss, so we spent nearly a day searching for it and the thieving bear. We combed the tundra thoroughly, but it had disappeared into thin air.

Since the animal had already been tagged, Roy couldn't replace what he'd lost. His hunt was officially over. Being a true sportsman, he chalked his loss up to an unfortunate accident. His only consolation was that it would give him another great story to tell around the campfire.

After losing that day, my guide and I were up at the crack of dawn the next morning, ready to head to a different area to hunt. We glassed for hours and couldn't find any bulls, so we took a break for lunch. As we sat there chatting, I heard a crack. Before I could take the sandwich out of my mouth, a forty-inch bull moose stepped out of the pine trees five yards in front of me.

Both of us froze like statues. My weapon lay useless beside me on the ground and we were at the mercy of this huge animal. The moose passed in front of us, giving us the once-over before continuing on without a care in the world. Once he was a safe distance away, my guide and I both breathed a sigh of relief.

This was not the most fabulous moment in my career. No hunter wants to be caught with a ham sandwich hanging out of his mouth and his gun on the ground when a 40-inch bull moose strolls right in front of him. The only thing soothing my hunter's pride was I didn't have a license to shoot a moose.

After lunch, we stopped every quarter mile and glassed. We walked for almost four hours. The going was not easy in tundra that contained a lot of bogs and areas with several water tributaries.

My guide had taken a gander to the left of me through his spotting scope, and I was listening to a sound I'd heard coming from my right. Suddenly, my guide tapped me on the shoulder and motioned to the bog out on the horizon. There stood a huge Woodland Caribou bull!

We needed to devised a plan quickly. I knew it would be a long chase, but he was such a regal bull I knew it would be worth it.

After checking the wind, we planned our first move. The bull was grazing out in the open, so we covered a quarter of a mile without haste and re-checked the animal's position. He was following a cow, and it looked like he was hot on her trail; she must have come into heat. That bull was *not* going to miss the opportunity to breed with her.

We closed the distance between us and the Caribou, and at 300 yards managed to get ahead of them. We were counting on them to crossing in front of us, so we covered 400 yards at the speed of lightning, or so it seemed at the time.

The cow led the beautiful bull like he was on a string. At 200 yards, I decided it was time to go for it. I set up and ranged him at 225 yards, then positioned the crosshairs of my scope on the bull's shoulders and squeezed the trigger.

Woodland Caribou bull harvested in Newfoundland, Canada using outfitter TRI-T Camps.

The shot punched through both shoulders, and he dropped right where he stood.

I was so happy. I'd finally shot a beautiful Woodland Caribou bull I could be proud of. I had accomplished yet another of the objectives in my overall plan.

The real work now commenced — capping, skinning, quartering and then backpacking the animal back to the boat with pack fames. It took two trips to get it all; he was a big boy.

✦   ✦   ✦

We hunters should always remember that hunting is a privilege and the animals we hunt deserve our respect. We should always be ethically correct in what we do in the outdoors, and stand up for what we love about it. For me, the outdoors is my sanctuary.

Caribou Meatballs in Onion Gravy

1-1/2 lb. Caribou shoulder	1 large egg, slightly beaten
1-1/4 cup loosely packed breadcrumbs	1/2 cup water
1/2 cup finely chopped celery	1-1/2 teaspoons salt
1/3 cup butter or margarine	Generous dash pepper
Marrow, if any	1/2 teaspoon poultry seasoning

Wipe meat with a clean damp cloth, trim off any strong smelling fat and remove bones. Grind meat twice. Reserve any marrow. Sauté celery in 2 tablespoons of butter for 10 minutes, then add to meat along with breadcrumbs, marrow and the remaining ingredients except butter. Mix thoroughly. Shape into small meatballs about 1 inch in diameter. Brown in the remaining butter quickly; lower heat and cook over medium heat for 10 minutes. Add onion gravy and simmer 2 minutes. Makes 3 to 3-1/2 dozen small meatballs.

Serves 6 to 8.

Onion Gravy

1-1/2 tablespoons flour	1 cup thinly sliced onions (2 medium)
2 tablespoons butter	1 cup finely shredded lettuce
1 cup water	
1/2 teaspoon salt	

Combine flour and melted butter in a skillet and stir over medium heat until mixture is browned (not scorched); add water gradually and cook until mixture is smooth and thick; stir constantly. Add remaining ingredients, cover and simmer for 15 minutes.

BAGGING 2 POPE & YOUNG QUALIFYING QUÉBEC-LABRADOR CARIBOU

I began my research about the Québec-Labrador Caribou with the study of their population in each area I was interested in hunting, as well as their migration patterns over the last couple of years. That finished, I researched and chose a great outfitter, Jack Hume.

Through my experience as both a hunter and booking agent, I've learned that the more you know, the more you'll increases your chances for success. This time around, I was acting as my own booking agent, so I called Jack and booked the trip on the spot.

When that was set, I called a few of my buddies to ask if they wanted to join me in a great Québec-Labrador Caribou hunt. Of course, they all answered in the affirmative.

Also joining this epic adventure were great hunters and my friends, Johnny S and Tommy T.

Everyone made arrangements, and before we knew it we were our way to the airport. We flew out of New York to Schefferville, Quebec. On arrival, we were greeted by the staff who assisted us with our gear and got the float plane loaded so we could head to a remote spike tent camp.

One hour later, we were settled in our tents. We ate supper and decided to take a boat ride to scout for game for the next morning. The tundra was beautiful. I'd never seen so many streams and lakes. We had, indeed, entered Caribou country.

Morning came early; none of us got much sleep because we were so excited to begin our quest. My guide and I loaded gear into our boat and headed out. I realized that no matter where you go in this area, you need a boat because there are so many lakes, rivers and streams.

Phenomenal outfitter success is not measured by how many animals are harvested, but by the memories the hunters make.

I'm guessing it took 30 minutes to reach the end of the lake, then we motored up a river tributary. A short time later, we beached the boat, and climbed up to a high peak where we saw some fair-sized Caribou roughly a mile and a half away.

Once we moved closer, we could see 400 Caribou walking in a straight line that covered a quarter of a mile. The wind was blowing out of the west, making conditions perfect for us to stalk our prey.

Traversing the tundra was not easy; there were bogs and water pockets everywhere. The trek to get in front of the herd took two and a half hours, but fate was with us because the Caribou grazed at a lazy pace.

There wasn't much cover in the tundra, so we had to be picky about finding an appropriate area to hide. The position we found was great, because we could view the Caribou as they passed within bow range.

I was using my Fred Bear Polar LTD bow that had Lemonwood limbs. It didn't even have cams, it had wheels! I used eastern arrows with Fred Bear fixed two blade broadhead arrowheads, which have two cutting surfaces. I'd sighted it in before I left, and after I got into camp I had re-checked my bow to make sure it was ready.

I was facing my moment of truth, so I hunkered down in the cover and waited. It looked like the migration might go right past me. I hoped the herd would travel close enough for me to seal the deal.

> **Caribou have a scent gland in their feet that allows them to follow each other through the tundra without getting lost.**

At 11:45, my dreams unraveled. The Caribou headed right to where I sat. I allowed the first 20 or 30 of them to walk right by me. I really wanted to shoot a mature bull. Time passed, and so did the Caribou. They changed course time after time, but I didn't see one I considered worthy of my arrow.

At the end of that long day, we packed up our gear, trudged back to the boat, and went back to camp. My friends had all had a terrific day — they each got a good Caribou, filling two of their tags. They planned to go out on day two to finish their second tags.

On day two, my guide and I navigated the same route and returned to the high summit to glass from the same location as the day before. We saw a band of several Caribou swim through a lake, and watched them exit on the opposite side of the lake.

We noticed a second herd entering the lake, so we hurried to the end of the lake to head them off before they exited in same place as the first herd. We set up a perfect ambush spot on the opposite side of the lake.

Of the 40 caribou, most were cows, but ten of them looked like outstanding bulls. Two of these bulls were headed in my direction, so I prepared to get off a shot. The first once passed 10 yards from me, so I felt confident bull number two would follow. I drew back my bow from a kneeling position, let my arrow fly, and hit the mark.

My guide crawled up to me and pointed as bull number five cruised past us. I barely had time to fetch an arrow from my quiver. When he was 18 yards in front of me, I drew my bow back to full draw and released the arrow. It slid right

One of two Québec-Labrador Caribou harvested in Schefferville, Québec, Canada. Both made Pope & Young.

into the animal's heart. Just like that, I'd harvested two great bulls in 20 minutes, both outstanding enough to make Pope & Young's standards.

My guide and I skinned both bulls and carried the quarters to the boat. My guide made two trips to camp because there was so much meat that the weight was too much for the boat if he tried to take it all at once.

I stayed behind and watched the sun set. The glorious colors allowed me to re-live the day's adventure. As darkness fell, my guide came back to pick me up and shared the the good news that all of my friends had filled their tags, too.

Back at camp we had a celebratory dinner of Caribou backstraps, roasted potatoes, fresh veggies, and let's not forget the pie. The three of us hardcore hunters had taken six great caribou on this trip. It was truly an epic memory.

Caribou Stew Deluxe

Marinade:
2 cups red wine (Burgundy or Claret)
1/4 cup cider vinegar
2 juniper berries cut in fourths
1 teaspoon salt

1/4 teaspoon whole black pepper
1 medium bay leaf
1/2 medium onion, sliced
1/2 small carrot, sliced
2 whole cloves

Stew:
2-1/2 lb. Caribou shoulder
3 tablespoons shortening
1/2 teaspoon pepper
1-1/8 teaspoons salt

1 medium onion, sliced
1/2 cup puréed tomatoes
3/4 cup water
1 tablespoon flour

Wipe meat with a clean damp cloth, trim off any strong smelling fat, then cut into two-inch cubes. Place in a glass or enamelware pan or bowl and pour the cold marinate over the meat. Turn the meat in the marinade twice daily. Marinate at least 24 hours, going longer for richer flavor.

When ready to cook, lift the meat out to drain on paper towel to prevent too much splattering when browning. Heat shortening in an aluminum kettle or skillet (iron may give a dark color) and brown the meat slowly on all sides. Add 3/4 cup of the strained marinade, pepper and salt. Cover and simmer gently for 1-1/2 hours. Then add onion, tomatoes and 1/2 cup water and continue to simmer for another hour. Thicken the sauce with flour blended into a smooth paste in remaining 1/4 cup of water. Boil 2 minutes longer.

Serves 6.

Grilled Marinated Caribou Sirloin

2-1/2 cups Caribou sirloin, trimmed and cut into 2-inch cubes
3/4 cup olive oil
1/2 cup honey
1/4 cup red wine vinegar
1/3 cup low-sodium soy sauce

1 tablespoon garlic powder
1-1/2 teaspoons ground ginger
1-1/2 teaspoons kosher salt
1 tablespoon freshly ground black pepper

Combine all ingredients aside from caribou into a tight-fitting jar and shake vigorously. Can be stored in the refrigerator for several weeks.

Place caribou in a non-reactive container or zip-lock bag. Add marinade, toss and refrigerate for 1-6 hours.

When ready to cook, remove from marinade, drain and place on a medium-high, well-oiled grill and brown on all sides, preferably not past medium-rare (130-135°F internal temperature).

Serves 4.

RECORD BREAKING UTAH MOUNTAIN LION

I was training at a fever pitch in preparation for my trip to the Book Cliff Mountains in Utah with Jerry Borden, who is a great outfitter. This time, the quarry would be a Mountain Lion. Jerry told me it would be a demanding hunt, and I would be hanging around with a fast-running crowd.

I was made to understand that these high-energy hunters could cover ground like a fast-moving freight train. So, I'd been training every day, including jogging five miles every other day for almost eight weeks. I was all in.

✦　✦　✦

I boarded a plane in Long Island, New York, bound for Utah. Jerry met me at the gate when I arrived and helped me get all my gear to his house, where I'd stay for the night.

I'd chosen Jerry for this hunt because he had a great reputation for hunting Mountain Lions. He'd spent the last 20 years chasing these beautiful cats. He was also an honorable man, which I respected.

They say that behind every great man is a woman. This was true in Jerry's case as well — his wife, Joyce, acted as his right hand. Not only did she cook for the hunters, she was also a cowboy's wife who was always there for her man.

When I first met Jerry, he asked me not make a face when I met his wife. He also begged me not to stare at her, even though she was extremely ugly. I agreed but was puzzled by his requests.

We got to his house and I got my gear unloaded just as we could see headlights coming up the driveway. Jerry reminded me about my promises, and my anxiety increased. When Joyce stepped out of the truck, I was shocked. She was one of the most beautiful women I've ever seen. The joke was on me, and we all had a good laugh.

The following morning dawned crisp and cold, with a hint of snow in the air. Jerry and I pulled out some topographical maps and mapped out our route to the Book Cliff Mountains. It promised to be a beautiful trip. The terrain reminded me of some parts of the Rocky Mountains.

We drove down many a logging road that first day, but we had no luck. After covering a lot of country, we gave up for the day and headed back to Jerry's house.

As the sun rose on day two, we loaded the dogs into the truck, topped off with fuel and set out for the day. After hours of driving, we finally saw fresh tracks in the dirt at 11 a.m. and stopped to check them out. From the looks of them, they'd been made by a big cat.

By this time, the dogs were going so crazy we could barely get the special radio collars on them before turning them loose. The radio collars would allow us to keep track of where the dogs were so we could find them. We also left one radio collar in the truck on the rearview mirror so we find our way back.

We climbed over rocks and up and down the mountain. It felt like I crawled over hundreds of downed trees at a dead run, trying to keep up with the dogs. We heard the dogs stop and figured they'd chased the cat up a tree, but by the time we got there, the wily lion had got down and sprinted of range.

By now, night was setting in. There was no stopping the dogs, though, so we kept going too. Eventually, we heard them howling from a quarter of a mile away. I won't kid you, at this point that quarter of a mile seemed like it was a million miles away. We'd been on the trail for 12 hours — I was wiped out!

This cat had more stamina than any animal or person I'd ever seen. He just kept going and going. I was amazed the dogs hadn't given up a long time ago. I decided if the dogs were still at it, then I had to be too.

By 4 a.m., we were struggling to figure out a way to catch up with the dogs. We were traveling on old horse trails, and in some cases old logging roads, but we couldn't get to where the dogs were. It was too dark for us to find our way.

The dogs finally trapped the cat in a tall pine tree. It was still too dark for humans to see, so we knew we'd need to wait for dawn's early light. The cat wasn't going anywhere. He felt as secure as could be up in his pine tree.

I felt like all the training I'd done for this trip hadn't even come close to preparing me for the pace the cat set. Every bone in my body ached, and my head felt like it was going to explode because of the dogs' incessant baying. I was almost ready to give up.

But as light slowly filled the sky, my determination returned. We lumbered over to where the dogs were still howling and I pulled out my 70-pound bow, while breathing like an Arkansas mule. I got to within 40 yards of the tree, but I didn't see the cat; it was more than 80 feet up.

The waiting game had now commenced. Finally, at 9 a.m. the beautiful cat moved. I spent precious moments judging how best to take the shot. I had my arrow ready, but struggled to reach full draw. Once I hit my anchor point, I let the arrow fly. The cat sprang up and performed a flip, but I still hit him! He hung on for 30 seconds before falling to the ground.

Jerry and I couldn't believe how big this majestic Mountain Lion was. Not only was this the biggest lion Jerry had ever hunted, it turned out to be the biggest and oldest lion the Colorado Fish & Wildlife Conservation Office had ever recorded. The person on duty that day said he could only guess at the cat's age, estimating him to be at least 16-1/2 years old. This guess was partly because the cat had no canine teeth in its upper jaw. The scars on his face indicated he had been a true scrapper.

The Mountain Lion harvested in Book Cliff Mountains in Utah was the biggest and oldest the Colorado Fish & Wildlife Conservation Office had ever recorded. It ended up being the number-one lion in the state that year, It scored a 16 inches green score, made Pope & Young and was eligible for Book and Crokett as well.

My mountain lion ended up being the number one lion in the state that year, scoring a 16-inch green score, according to Pope & Young. Not only did my lion make Pope & Young, he was also eligible for Boone and Crockett.

I will always remember that hunt in the Book Cliff Mountains and that amazing Mountain Lion. I had a life-sized mount made of him and it has a place of pride in my trophy room.

Two years after this epic hunt, my good friend Jerry Boren passed away, leaving a massive hole in my heart. I will always recall the smile on Jerry's face when we harvested that enormous old cat. Giants are not measured by their size but rather by how they affect your life, and Jerry certainly was a giant in my eyes.

The following year a woman named Kitty from the National Rifle Association contacted me say one of the highest awards in the National Rifle Association had been bestowed upon me, the Leather Stocking Award. This award was given to me in the archery category. I dedicated the award to Jerry Boren, for without him, I would not have had this adventure of a lifetime.

Mountain Lion Meatballs Stuffed with Cheese

2-1/2 cups Mountain Lion, trimmed and cut into 2-inch cubes
3/4 cup olive oil
1/2 cup honey
1/4 cup red wine vinegar
1/3 cup low-sodium soy sauce
1 tablespoon garlic powder
1-1/2 teaspoons ground ginger
1-1/2 teaspoons kosher salt
1 tablespoon freshly ground black pepper

Mix meat with all ingredients except cheese and oil. Make small balls of the mixture, then insert a piece of cheese inside each.

Refrigerate for one hour minimum.

Pour oil into a frying pan and heat it until oil shimmers. Drop meatballs into oil one by one and fry until they are brown and crisp.

Sweet and Sour Lion

1/2 pound Mountain Lion tenderloin, cut into bite-sized pieces

2 rings of pineapple, diced

1/2 each yellow, red and green bell pepper

1 clove garlic, minced

Oil for frying

Marinade:

1 teaspoon soy sauce

Rice wine to cover meat

1-2 teaspoons of corn starch

Batter:

1/2 cup water

2 tablespoons flour

1 tablespoon corn starch

1/2 teaspoon baking soda

1 egg

1 teaspoon oil

Sauce:

1-1/2 tablespoon ketchup

1 teaspoon plum sauce

1/4 teaspoon Worcester-shire sauce

1 teaspoon oyster sauce

1 teaspoon cornstarch

1 teaspoon sugar

Mix batter, coat meat and fry in a large skillet or wok. Set aside and drain most of the oil.

Brown garlic , then add peppers and pineapple. Heat for 5-10 minutes.

Mix sauce ingredients and add to pan. Heat until thickened.

Serve over steamed rice.

COLORADO MULE DEER, FINALLY

The Mule Deer is an exciting quarry and doesn't really compare to a white-tailed deer, even though it has similar habits. The habitat of the mule deer is different from the white-tailed deer because it appreciates the arid plains, like the antelope. The Mule Deer also loves the hills and the draws in canyons and open fields.

I commenced my hunt for the Mule Deer by studying the states that issue mule deer permits, and by talking to conservation officers to find out which state offered the best chance for me to harvest a prize. I was looking for a typical 4 x 4, which is 4 points on each set of horns. After much research, I decided I wanted my Mule Deer challenge to take place in Colorado — the state had several Mule Deer and had produced some record animals.

Once I selected Colorado, I narrowed it down to one county where I could search for the outfitter who had the best knowledge of the area so he could help me meet my goal.

The area I selected in Colorado had a draw system in place, so I had to apply to the state for a license. If I wasn't picked, I'd get a preference point for the next year. Ultimately, I had to wait three years before I was finally selected — good thing I had those preference points!

In June I received notice that I'd been awarded a mule deer tag in the northeast corner of Colorado. The first thing on my to-do list was to check out the hunting season dates, to make sure I'd be able to hunt during opening week of the season.

I chose my date, got my plane ticked and picked a guide, Tommy T. When that was done, I made my list of gear and checked everything to make sure it was in tip-top shape. Then, I packed and was ready to go.

One of my closest friends, Jim C, with whom I had hunted for many years, planned to join me on this trip. Jim hails from Long Island, and is an accomplished hunter and die-hard athlete. He even completed an Ironman triathlon in Hawaii.

When the day finally came, I met Jim at Islip airport on Long Island, at the crack of dawn. A short time later, we arrived in Colorado, where the weather punched us in the face as we got off the plane.

This trip was an emotional one for me, and Jim was doing a good job of keeping me company. Three months prior to this trip, I'd lost the greatest thing God had given me, my beautiful wife. Cancer had claimed her life. Jim was my truest hunting buddy, and helped me get back on track after that devastating loss. I will always treasure his friendship.

We grabbed something to eat on our way to the motel we were going to call home for the next week. I was excited to hear that Tommy had seen some promising Mule Deer the day before we arrived.

Early the next morning, we loaded up two jeeps and headed to one of Tom's private farms. We split into two groups, Jim and another gentleman went to one end of the farm, while Tom and I stayed on the other end. We thought having two groups and covering more ground would give us a better chance.

I took my trusty daypack out of the Jeep and made one final check to make sure that I had my license and all the equipment I needed for the day. Then, we were off.

We saw some young Mule Deer initially, but they were just too small. Later through binoculars we saw a mature buck. He showed nice presence, so we put on a stalk.

We hiked for two miles and maneuvered ourselves into position, which was approximately 400 yards from a Mule

Deer that looked like a 170 class. I took out my old spotting scope and judged the animal for maturity as best I could. After 20 minutes of watching him and thinking about it, I passed on this guy. He was mature, but needed another year or two to grow.

Before I participate in a hunt, I go to the record books. One of the key factors I take into consideration when I judge an animal is its maturity. I looked at picture after picture to see what a mature Mule Deer looked like. I studied the animal from every angle, and I knew exactly what I wanted. Now all I had to do was find it.

Day one ended with a great meal and no Mule Deer for me. After dinner, we talked about the terrain and the number of deer we'd seen.

We embarked on day two and hadn't even been out for an hour of stalking when we encountered five bucks tending eight does. But, again, none of them were what I considered mature enough.

We traveled far and wide all day, but never spotted what I was looking for.

Day three started off slow. Tommy and I ventured into a different section of the ranch. Tom's property was a working cattle ranch on the north section and a working farm on the south. Tommy and I took a crack at a far off rugged area.

We'd been glassing with our binoculars and a spotting scope for an hour when I finally found the Mule Deer I wanted. Tom looked at it through his binoculars and was speechless. He'd been guiding for more than 20 years, and for the first time he was seeing a once-in-a-lifetime Mule Deer. It was a behemoth!

The deer was 400 yards or so below us, and we watched him as he bedded down with a doe. We crawled on our bellies for approximately 200 yards and set up on a grassy knoll. I didn't know Jimmy was on the opposite side of the canyon on a ridge 500 yards away from the Mule Deer I had my sights on. He got to watch everything unfold as I made my final set up before making my play.

We lay there on our bellies for three hours, watching. Tommy must've asked me three or four times if I was sure I could make the shot. Even though we'd sighted in our rifles when we arrived, he'd only seen me shoot a target at 100 yards — this was 350, and he was worried.

A strong wind was blowing from east to west at that time. As time passed, the impressive buck stood and faced downhill. This made for a difficult shot.

It was time for a Texas hotshot. If you've never heard of this, it's where you aim at the rear end of a deer and hope for the best. The placement of your shot must be perfect in the rear of the animal so that the bullet travels the complete length of the body cavity and exits through the front.

I allowed for the wind and squeezed the trigger. The deer took off. Tom thought I'd missed him. I asked Tom to work his way back to the truck while I went to see if I could find my deer.

The day was hot and dry, and for the first time, I second-guessed my shot. I hiked the 350 yards to the spot where I'd last seen him, but I saw no sign of a hit — no blood trail. So, I did the next best thing and followed the deer's tracks on the ground. One thing I'd learned over the years was the dirt never lies.

So, I followed the story written there, but the ground showed no sign that the deer had been hit. I walked another 35 yards, and I realized my quest was over. There in the dirt lay the most beautiful Mule Deer anyone could ever harvest. Since this was my first, I was amazed by the size of the rack on this one.

I heard the truck on the top of the ridge, and could see Tommy coming down the slope to where I sat. He took one look at my Mule Deer and was struck dumb. He suggested I was looking at a Boone and Crockett record book animal. In 20 years of guiding, it was Tommy's first Boone and Crockett-level animal.

I was never one for record books, but I always appreciated great animals. Tommy made me promise I would have this Mule Deer scored. I did as he asked, and it had a green score of 204. After the 60-day drying period, he scored 197.

This Mule Deer harvested in Colorado had a green score of 204, with a 197 after the 60-day drying period. It was one for the Boone and Crockett record books.

Tommy later confided that the Mule Deer is one of the hardest animals to put in the record books.

I must thank my lifelong friend Jimmy for going with me on this hunting adventure. Though he watched the action unfold through a pair of binoculars, I knew he was cheering for me.

Remember that every adventure has a beginning and an end. I always look at the end of one adventure as the opportunity to plan and the beginning my next one.

Sweet Mule Deer Sausage

10 lbs. mule deer trimmings
1 lb side bacon
3 lb pork loin
Montreal Steak Seasoning
Cumin seed
HY's Seasoning Salt without MSG or our favorite

seasoning salt
3/4 cup chopped garlic
1-1/2 cups processed honey (not the solid raw version)
Hot pepper flakes (optional)

Grind the mule deer, bacon, and pork through a medium screen, alternating chunks of mule deer meat with bacon and pork. On a clean flat surface, flatten the ground meat to the thickness of a pizza crust, then season liberally with the spices. Next, spoon dollops of garlic onto the meat and pour the honey over it all. Mix very well with your hands, using a kneading motion, until the mixture is as homogeneous as possible.

Take a small portion of the sausage mixture, make it into a patty, fry it over medium-high heat, and then taste it to see if you need to adjust the seasonings. Continue to do this until the sausage has the flavor you want.

Once you've achieved the desired flavor, either put it through the stuffer to make cased sausages, or package it up like burgers for country style sausages.

Mule Deer Sausage Bread

1 pound venison sausage	1 package fresh pizza
1 large package shredded	dough
mozzarella	1 tablespoon oregano
2 eggs	Marinara sauce (optional)

Preheat oven to 350 degrees.

Brown sausage, drain and let cool slightly. Combine mozzarella sausage and oregano. Whisk 2 egg whites and one egg yolk together, reserving the remaining yolk for later. Combine whisked eggs with sausage mixture.

Press dough onto greased cookie in a rectangular shape. Spoon mixture into middle of dough and bring long sides together in the middle and fold together. Crimp ends. Place seam side down on greased baking sheet and brush the top with the remaining egg yolk.

Bake for 30 minutes or until crust is golden brown. Remove from oven and cool slightly before serving.

Great dipped in marinara sauce.

FACING THE CHALLENGE OF AN ARCTIC MUSKOX HUNT

If you love cold weather and a brutal environment, this hunt has your name written all over it. My journey to hunt a Muskox began when I watched a National Geographic show that told all about the animal. After learning about it, I just knew I had to harvest one.

The challenge for me surrounding this hunt was the unknown — I had no idea what the weather would be like and how it would affect my archery equipment. Although I always prepare for every hunt, I didn't know how to effectively prepare for the bitter cold I'd be facing.

I booked this trip with Guided Arctic Expeditions and bough my airline tickets. I planned to hunt on Banks Island, off the coast of British Columbia in Canada. The countdown to cold had begun.

With all the gear and cold weather clothing required, I felt like I was packing for a 40-day trip, instead of the 14 days I'd reserved.

I arrived on Banks Island, and stepping off the plane into the -10° weather was a shock. The biggest challenge on this hunt was going to be not freezing to death.

The following morning, a bunch of howling dogs woke me. When I looked outside, I saw it was snowing like hell. I told myself I was ready.

My Inuit guide, Roy Goose, greeted me and helped load the equipment onto snowmobiles. The snowmobiles revved, and sled dogs jerked on their harnesses to get started. Today, a long snow sled would be my limousine.

Joining me on this expedition was my good friend Tom, who was also my cameraman. He was going to try to capture my whole hunt on film.

The thermometer read –15°, and the wind was blowing hard across the tundra. As we set off, I was amazed to learn that the Inuit travel according to the sun rather than using a compass.

We glided over the frozen tundra all day, stopping at 4 p.m. to set up a tent camp. By this time, it was –20° and the temperature would continue to drop throughout the night. We planned to sleep on the ice, or to be more precise the arctic ocean, so the Inuits set up small tents and then laid muskox pelts hair side down to be the barrier between us and the ice. We also used muskox pelts as blankets.

For the first time in my life, I slept with all my clothes on. Even though thick muskox hides covered me, and the Coleman stove ran nonstop, I still nearly froze to death. None of us got much sleep.

We were up by 4 a.m., which wasn't a problem since it never really gets dark there this time of year. It's why this place is called the land of the midnight sun. I had to pee in the worst way, and I felt like I won first place in a track meet for the fastest-man-to-pee event.

The early morning temperature was −25°, and I was worried about my bow and how it would perform in these brutal conditions. I'd sighted it in at home, where it was 50° outside. The temperature here could fall to −50° with the windchill, and my bow had wood limbs. I just had no clue how it would react in this cold, so I sighted it again there in camp.

Day two would be our first day of hunting. We didn't see any Muskox but we did see two polar bears, which was unbelievable. That afternoon, I harvested an arctic hare, and our dinner menu was set. Cooking in this hostile environment was a chore. For example, it takes water forever to boil. Despite this, we had some superb meals on the trip.

✦　✦　✦

On day three the actual temperature hoovered at –25°, and I didn't want to know the windchill. Breathing took its toll, and ice hung off my mustache down to the end of my goatee. I sometimes had to break the ice between my mustache and my goatee just so I could open my mouth.

Our guide wanted to go out to inspect a certain area and asked Tom and me to stay behind. An hour later, I saw two Muskox through my binoculars. Since I was in total hunt mode, I decided to check them out, even though it had started to snow.

My guide, Roy, returned just after I left and was not happy with me leaving. He quickly caught up with me and explained, in a nice way, how dangerous it was. If there had been a white out, I never would have been able to find my way back and most likely would have perished. I was grateful to him for the lesson and vowed to be more careful from that point forward.

The Muskox I'd seen was still in the vicinity, so I fetched my bow and stalked him through the ice floes, using them for cover so I could get close enough to close the deal. The animal hadn't seen me yet, but time and distance were not in my favor.

I got to within 30 yards of where he nibbled the permafrost,scavenging for food. I drew my bow back and took a shot. My biggest fear came true when the arrow sailed underneath him. My fingers were freezing and not releasing like they should. Next, I placed my sight pin on the back of the Muskox to compensate for my fingers, and let my second arrow fly.

It didn't seem like the arrow penetrated this guy's pelt very deeply. These animals have extremely high-density pelts — they have to be tough to live in such a savage environment — so it was going to be difficult to achieve my goal.

I grabbed another arrow and made a follow-up shot. Although I took two good shots, I still couldn't believe the animal's stamina as he ran across the tundra. He traveled about 70 yards, and then dropped to the frozen Artic floor.

At that point, I could barely feel my fingers, face and ears. I hadn't even felt the cold, though, until after the Mus-

Harvesting this muskox earned my second Leather Stocking Award from the National Rifle Association.

kox expired. My teeth were chattering, but I knew I'd forget about my discomfort once the real work started.

If you've never skinned an animal as big as a Muskox, try doing it at –25°! Roy told me the windchill made it feel like –55 to –65°. This ordeal was unlike anything I'd experienced before.

Nature can be cruel, but at the same time quite beautiful. The beauty of this frozen expanse and the wonder of the animals that live there were an added bonus on this hunt.

The Muskox was another record-breaker, and the National Rifle Association awarded me my second Leather Stocking Award in the archery classification for this harvest.

Stuffed Muskox Tenderloin with Cranberry Coulis

4 ounces Muskox tenderloin, butterflied and slightly pounded
1 mushroom, sliced

2 ounces Swiss cheese, thinly sliced
4 small broccoli florets

Cranberry Coulis
4 tablespoons fresh cranberries

2 teaspoons orange juice, fresh squeezed

Side Dish
1 tablespoon butter
1/2 clove garlic, finely minced assorted fresh vegetables

1 medium potato, boiled
2 tablespoons lemon juice

Preheat oven to 350°F.

Simmer the cranberries in the orange juice until they just start to burst. Set aside and keep warm.

Stuff the Muskox with the cheese, mushroom and broccoli and roll it up and tie it with string. Bake for 25 minutes at 350°F. Untie the muskox and top with cranberry coulis.

Serve with fresh vegetables sauteed in garlic butter and sprinkled with lemon juice.

Muskox Barley Soup

2 pounds Muskox meat
2 large onions, chopped
2 celery stalks, chopped
1 garlic clove
1 tablespoon butter
1/4 cup sherry

Basil to taste
Rosemary to taste
Bay leaf to taste
3-4 peppercorns
2 potatoes diced very small
1/2 cup barley

Cut meat into 1-inch cubes. Brown meat, onions and garlic clove butter.

When meat is browned, fill pot with water and add seasonings. Simmer for an hour or until meat is tender. Add barley and simmer.

Just before barley is done, add potatoes and cook just until potatoes are done.

10-YEAR WAIT FOR CANADIAN MOOSE

At this point, I'd been applying for a Moose tag in the State of Maine for more than 10 years, hoping I'd finally apply often enough to be chosen from the thousands of non-residents who apply each year. So far, it hadn't happened for me, but each year I was denied, I earned a preference point that would increase my chances of getting a tag the following year. The only other way I could get a tag was if someone who got one listed me as their subpermittee (alternate) and then transferred the tag to me.

My good friend Jeff, who had been applying for the lottery as a resident for almost 20 years, did just that. Jeff called in June, after I'd been passed by yet again, to tell me he'd finally been successful in drawing a Moose tag, but no longer wanted to use it. He was giving it to me and I was euphoric!

The permit was good for opening week, so in late August I reviewed my checklist to make sure I had all my gear. I also invited my good friend of 25 years, Joe Ferraro, to accompany me. He wanted to be there when I fulfilled my dream of harvesting a Moose.

✦ ✦ ✦

The location for this hunt was the upper Allagash region of Maine. For me, this was like getting an early Christmas present. The fall foliage was on spectacular display, and the leaves danced as each breath of wind brought a kaleidoscope of color raining down onto the forest floor. We stayed at Jeff's house, which was nestled in the picturesque town of Ashland. He had kindly offered to let us use his house as base camp for our daily trips afield.

We started out early each morning, jumping into Jeff's all-terrain vehicle and traversing the old logging roads in the area. We spent our time wending our way through the areas the logging companies had cleared.

We had to drive for an hour just to get to the place where my license allowed me to hunt. Once we got there, we walked logging roads and made cow calls to see if we could scare up an interested bull Moose. No luck.

I wasn't concerned about this. I'd never punched a tag on the first day of any of my hunting trips. It always seemed like Mother Nature wanted me to work for it! So, each trip I spend a good amount of time searching high and low for my target. Sometimes, it's the fifth, sixth, or seventh day before I get lucky. I've also been on trips where I came home empty-handed.

That's just the way it is. Not all trips can earn a successful harvest. I consider every trip a success, though, because I always come away with new knowledge and a stronger passion to push forward and achieve what I set out to do.

✦　✦　✦

Day two was a bit more productive. We saw quite a few cow Moose, which livened things up a bit for us. That afternoon, the wind blew hard and we ran the old logging roads looking for good Moose feeding grounds. While we were doing this, we encountered several other moose hunters doing the same thing.

Hunting hard is never an option, it's a necessity if you want to be successful, so we pushed forward. We kept at it until we ran out of daylight, then headed back to Jeff's.

✦　✦　✦

The alarm clock blared at me in the wee hours of the third day, and for the first time in my hunting career it was not a welcome sound. I rolled out of bed anyway, and proceeded to drink about a gallon of coffee before geting my gear together and heading out with Joe.

I felt more envigorated once we were rolling. I never get tired of seeing all the wonders nature has to offer.

After we'd been out walking for a while, we ran into a couple of hunters who had harvested a nice bull Moose. They were so excited. As fate would have it, we didn't get to join their ranks that day but we did spend a day enjoying the beauty of fall in the state of Maine.

✦ ✦ ✦

On day four, I'd regained my confidence. We traveled down many abandoned logging roads, calling the Moose every now and then, but we got no response. At, noon, we stopped for a homemade lunch, fixed right on the tailgate of the truck. It was one of the best lunches Joe and I had ever had.

At 1:30, we called some more and thought we heard a grunt. We exited the truck, and heard a snap not too far off in the woods. Encouraged, we headed down an old logging road on foot and then heard another snap.

The next thing we knew, out stepped a beautiful bull Moose right in front of us. I dropped to my knees and let my Winchester 70 .375 HH do the talking for me. I didn't have time to judge the Moose, I just slowly squeezed the trigger and made my shot. It looked good, but the animal bounded off the road and into a swamp.

I was confident in my shot, so I waited for half an hour until I thought I heard him fall. We then waded into the swamp and definitely heard a crash.

We splashed through the bog, up to our knees in brackish water, weaving through dead trees that littered the area. Jeff followed the blood trail and was ahead of Joe and me by almost a hundred yards. Joe had twisted his ankle the previous day and was using a walking stick I'd whittled for him, which made for slow going in this treacherous terrain.

Suddenly, I heard three beautiful words come out of Jeff's mouth, "You got him!"

When we finally caught up, Jeff was standing there showing me my beautiful 40-inch moose. (The measurement is made from the tip at the longest point of the antler on the left side to the tip at the longest point of the antler on the right side.) I was so proud — I'd never harvested a Moose before.I was amazed by the size of the animal. I would guess he weighed between 900 and 1,000 pounds.

Jeff, my guide, and I pose with my 40-inch Canadian moose.

Since I'd never skinned a moose, I didn't realize what a chore it would be. We worked at it for two solid hours without stopping, then had to cart it back to the vehicle. If anyone ever tells you a quarter of a moose isn't heavy — don't you believe them!

After two long trips, we managed to lug the moose out to the logging road. We loaded him into the pickup truck and took him to the check station to record his age and get the necessary paperwork to transport the animal out of state.

I took the hide to the local taxidermist, so he could flesh it out and take off any excess fat. He then salted it so the hair wouldn't slip and prepared it for my trip home.

When that was done, we returned to Jeff's house and cut up the meat. It turned out to be a long night, but it was also a fruitful one.

Processing the meat from a hunt is another facet in being a responsible hunter. Being able to supply food for your freezer so you can enjoy the bounty the harvested animal offers you is awesome.

Moose Sirloin Steak
with Sautéed Mushrooms and Red Wine Sauce

4 7-ounce Moose sirloin steaks, room temperature

2 tablespoons plus 1 teaspoon olive oil

Few dashes kosher salt

Dash of fresh ground pepper

2 tablespoons shallot (minced)

1 cup red wine

1/2 teaspoon coarsely ground pepper

1 cup beef stock (homemade or packaged, not canned)

6 tablespoons unsalted butter

10 ounces sliced white or brown mushrooms

Pat the steaks dry with paper towels and massage them with 2 tablespoons of olive oil. Liberally season both sides of the steaks with Kosher salt and freshly ground pepper:

Melt 1 tablespoon butter in a small saucepan over medium heat. Add the minced shallot, and sauté for 3 to 4 minutes until just starting to caramelize. Stir in the wine and pepper, and bring to a low boil. Let it reduced to 1/2 cup, about 10 minutes. Stir in the beef stock and bring it to a low boil, letting it reduce half again, about 10 more minutes. The sauce should now be shiny with a deep rich brown color. Remove from heat. (You can prepare the sauce ahead of time and re-warm it.)

Preheat oven to 450° F. Melt 1 tablespoon of butter in a heavy skillet over medium heat. When the foam subsides, add the sliced mushrooms. Sprinkle them with salt and pepper, and cook until golden brown. Transfer to a plate with slotted spoon.

Continued on next page

Moose Sirloin Steak (CONTINUED)

Heat 2 tablespoons butter and 1 teaspoon of olive oil in the same skillet over medium-high heat. When the foam subsides, add the Moose steaks and brown both sides, 2 minutes per side.

Transfer the skillet to the preheated oven, and roast the steaks 8 to 10 minutes, depending on the thickness, to medium-rare. (Take care to not over-cook, as the meat dries out easily.)

Take the skillet out of the oven and pour the cooking juices from the steaks into the sauce. Rewarm the sauce over low heat and whisk in the 2 remaining tablespoons butter, one-half tablespoon at a time, until the sauce takes on a satiny sheen.

To serve, scatter some mushrooms over each moose steak, and drizzle the sauce on top and around each steak.

AOUDAD BECOMES 6TH SHEEP IN MY COLLECTION

When I finished my Moose hunt, I was ready for some rest and relaxation. That wasn't to be, though, because a friend called me and asked me to join him and a few others in Texas to hunt Aoudad Sheep. The guys proposed a five-day getaway. Since we were in between seasons, I decided this would be a great way to let off some steam.

I planned to hunt with a good friend of mine, Steve Jones, who is an outfitter in South Texas and New Mexico. I knew from experience, hunting with Steve would be fun.

✦　✦　✦

Steve met me and my friend, Joe Ferraro, at the airport in New Mexico, and from there we drove for an hour and a half to the camp. Steve, Joe and I sat around the campfire that afternoon, drank a few beers, and ate chili peppers stuffed with game meat and wild onions.

After we ate, Steve told us about the Aoudad Sheep, the terrain where they lived, and their feeding habits. This sheep is a hearty breed, and spends its whole life among the jagged rocks and cliffs.

Our first day of the hunt was spent touring different parts of the ranch where we'd be hunting. I was amazed by how rocky and hilly the terrain was, not to mention how steep. We encountered both lush valleys and rugged rocky areas. As the day wore on, we realized just how big the ranch actually was.

We saw herds of antelope, a lot of armadillos, and quite a few javelina (medium-sized animals that resemble a wild boar). We covered a great deal of territory that day, but didn't see any Aoudad Sheep.

The weather didn't cooperate with us on our second day out. It poured from the minute we got up on into the wee hours of the next morning. Our solution? We were forced to have several cold beers and sit around jacking our jaws — a terrible job, but somebody had to do it!

On day three, Steve took us to a new section of the ranch. This territory was extremely steep and featured rocky canyons. I lost my footing on the way down one exceptionally steep grade, and fell roughly 10 feet. I landed on a bunch of rocks and was okay, but my rifle wasn't. My scope was damaged, which brought my hunting to an early close for the day. I didn't want to risk shooting a rifle that might have other, hidden damage.

We drove back to camp, and I told Steve what happened. He graciously said I could borrow one of his rifles. I appreciated that, but using someone else's rifle is difficult because you don't know anything about it.

So, off to the shooting range I went. The borrowed gun was a 7mm. I fired approximately 20 rounds at 100 yards, and sighted it in two inches high, the same as my rifle.

Feeling comfortable with the borrowed firearm, I devised a new game plan for the following day with my cohorts. We intended to return to the rocky canyon, because it looked like the perfect spot to find some sheep.

I was confident the next morning as I set out with my borrowed rifle. Not long after we left, I noticed a ewe grazing on the hillside, about 500 yards from where we were using binoculars to glass the rugged terrain.

Once we'd seen her, we hiked for a time and got in position, approximately 250 yards from the sheep. Steve and I had been hunting as a team, but decided to split up now so we could cover more ground. We'd meet in an hour to compare notes.

I went to the east, and he went to the west. I'd covered about a quarter of a mile, when I saw Steve working his way back toward me. I peered down a canyon that was about 200 yards deep and saw a magnificent sheep grazing there.

We had plenty of time to set up, since the wind was blowing in our favor. The sheep had no idea we were there. We closed the distance to approximately 150 yards.

At this distance, I didn't have to worry about making the shot, so we set up behind an outcropping of rocks. I steadied my rifle and waited for the sheep to move. When he was in position, I used my scope to position the shot just behind his shoulders, and then squeezed the trigger.

I made a great shot, and the sheep took off, but he didn't go far. We found him 80 yards away.

He had great bases and a beautiful set of horns, which made me happy. He was the sixth sheep in my collection. I paid respect to this wonderful animal; he'd created another wonderful deposit in my memory bank.

HUNT HARD   HUNT SAFE

Me posing with my beautiful Aoudad sheep.

Slow-Cooked Aoudad Sheep Curry

1 Aoudad backstrap, cubed
    in large chunks
6-8 tablespoons curry
    powder
1 tablespoon allspice
2 onions, chopped)
1 ginger root
6-7 cloves garlic

1 jalapeño pepper, chopped
1 can coconut milk
1 can diced tomatoes
1 teaspoon thyme
1 teaspoon cayenne pepper
1 teaspoon garlic powder
Vegetable oil

Mix garlic powder, cayenne pepper, and 1 tablespoon curry and sprinkle cubed meat. Cook diced onions and ginger slightly and then add meat and lightly brown. Remove the meat and let it rest in a bowl.

Dice 1 onion, ginger, and 4-6 cloves of garlic. Place in blender or food processor and blend until the mixture is smooth.

Place Aoudad meat, blended mixture, diced tomatoes, coconut milk, jalapeño and two cups of water in slow cooker. Add thyme, allspice, and remaining curry and stir together. Cook on low for 6-8 hours, or until meat is fork-tender.

Serve with mashed potatoes, rice or roasted root vegetables.

DALL SHEEP IS FIRST IN MY
NORTH AMERICAN GRAND SLAM

A s I thought about hunting the Dall Sheep, I knew this would be a physically challenging proposition. Hunting sheep always comes at a high cost for both the hunter and the sheep.

Once I made up my mind to do it, I set my sights on Alaska. I also upped the stakes by deciding to attempt the North American Grand Slam. This meant I'd have to harvest four varieties of sheep: Dall, Stone, Bighorn and Desert.

My choice for an outfitter for this trip was easy — Mel Gillis, a good friend and renowned sheep hunter. We would be hunting from a remote outpost camp in the Wrangell Mountains. My son, Scott, and my good friend Jimmy would join me on this adventure.

✦ ✦ ✦

We all arrived in Fairbanks, where Mel and my guide, Chris, greeted us. I took a long, hard look at Chris and had a feeling he was going to whip me into shape ove the next 10 days. This guy looked lean, mean and ready for whatever the mountains could throw at him.

We loaded our bags into Mel's truck and headed to an airstrip, where we met our pilot, Joel. The Cessna 180 was soon loaded, and away we flew. The flight to our camp took an hour. As we crossed the Wrangle Mountains, I got a good look at just how rugged they are.

We landed on a gravel bar runway that ran alongside the Copper River. We loaded our gear onto a few four-wheelers and spent the night in a log cabin. As usual when hunting, a cook served us a superlative dinner, which that night happened to be wild sheep and roasted potatoes. We all hit the sack early, but I couldn't sleep and spent most of the night thinking about the hunt.

We were up early, and breakfast was a quick affair — all I wanted to do was hunt and I was ready to get started. Before we could start the hunt, we had to backpack five miles upriver to a spike camp consisting of two tents in the middle of nowhere.

Scott coming along on this trip made it extra special because I wanted him to experience the great outdoors with me his first time out. I was looking forward to teaching him what I knew about hunting. Our guide, Chris, also contributed his knowledge and taught Scott a lot.

It took three hours to get to the camp. Once there, we set up our tents next to a stream, found some firewood, and built a fire. Soon after, Chris had a great dinner ready for us.

After dinner, we broke out our spotting scopes and binoculars and set to work formulating our plan of attack. It's always a good idea to have a plan when hunting sheep so you can figure out how to reach your quarry without being seen. Sheep have sharp eyesight and they can pick up movement from long distances, so a plan that implements sleath is required.

The next morning, anticipation was running high as we prepared to head out. The first thing on our agenda was to find a sheep from our tent camp. Mountains surrounded us on both sides of the river, so we used our spotting scopes and binoculars to search.

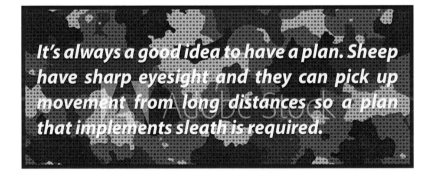

It's always a good idea to have a plan. Sheep have sharp eyesight and they can pick up movement from long distances so a plan that implements sleath is required.

We saw a flock, then spent an hour figuring out how to get up the mountain without them seeing us. The game was on!

There were 15 sheep grazing on the opposite side of the river, at the top of a mountain on a grassy slide. At 6 a.m., we grabbed our backpacks and climbed up to where we'd seen them.

It wasn't an easy trip, sometimes requiring climbing hand over hand, and trekking through exceptionally rugged terrain. A grueling seven hours later, we found ourselves directly across from the sheep.

I'd brought several white jumpsuits with me, so we each put one on to cover our final approach, hoping that the sheep would think we were one of them. We set up in a rock outcropping and glassed them. We waited there, hoping they would graze closer to us.

After being patient for three hours, we realized they weren't going to come to us. At this point, we were 10 hours into our stalk. As we prepared to move, I happened to look up and saw two rams standing 500 yards above us.

Our guide checked them out through his binoculars and realized one was legal, which meant he sported full curl horns (meaning they grew all the way around to meet his eye area). Chris looked at me with a question in his eyes, and I gave him a thumbs-up.

We moved 100 yards closer without being seen. We crawled the second 100 yards on our bellies. Finally, we narrowed the gap to 300 yards. It looked like a straight uphill shot from this vantage point. Breathing heavily and feeling like I'd just run a mile, I tried to get myself under control.

Chris mimed for me to take a minute and catch my breath before trying to make the shot. I took some deep breaths, and rested my rifle on my backpack. When my breathing was normal and I felt settled, I set up for the shot.

I set my sights on the ram, held my breath, then slowly exhaled and squeezed the trigger. The ram disappeared and showed no signs that my bullet had hit anywhere close to its mark.

Chris jumped up and yelled at me to look to the right. Sure enough, I saw my Dall Sheep fall and roll 800 yards down the mountainside. I was so damn happy, I jumped up and down like a school kid who got an A+ on his report card.

We made our way down to the ram, and saw that it was a beautiful specimen. We skinned and quartered the sheep and loaded up our backpacks with the meat once we'd finished the skinning.

Chris stowed the head and the hide into my backpack and told me to start down the mountain and follow the drainage basin (where two mountains meet forming a run off crease that deflects melting snow and rain down to streams and smaller tributaries below).

I thought going downhill would be a piece of cake compared to what we'd gone through to get to where we were. Boy, was I was wrong. The terrain was treacherous, espe-

Me with my Dall Sheep, the first in my North American Grand Slam.

cially when carrying a loaded backpack. It took me seven hours to get back to camp. I don't mind saying this: "That mountain kicked my ass!"

By the time I got back, I had 16 blisters on my feet. All told, it had taken more than 17 hours to complete this hunt.

When Chris arrived, about 30 minutes later, we radioed base camp and told them I had harvested a sheep. Jimmy, who was already at basecamp, said he'd harvested a sheep as well. When I told him about my blisters, he kindly walked five miles to bring me some medical supplies and see my sheep. Now that's true friendship.

Chris warmed water so I could soak my feet. He then popped all my blisters and told me to put my feet in the water. He'd forgotten to mention that he'd put salt in it. I lit up like a Christmas tree when that salty water hit all those blisters.

According to Chris, this treatment necessary. When they were done soaking, He covered my feet with moleskin and taped it in place so I'd be able to make the trek home.

I thanked Mel Gillis for helping me conquer the first leg of my grand slam — one down and three to go. I was also happy that Scott was with me so we could have this adventure of a lifetime.

Dall Sheep Chili

2 pounds of finely ground
  Dall Sheep meat
2 cups chili beans
1 can chopped tomatoes
1 can tomato sauce
1 cup water
1/2 cup chopped black olives
Salt to taste

1 to 1-1/2 teaspoons of red
  pepper
1 to 1-1/2 teaspoons of black
  pepper
Chili powder to taste
Chopped onions and
  shredded cheese for
  garnish

Pour all the ground sheep meat into a thick walled cooking pot, stir well and cook until browed. Drain grease and discard. Put meat back into pot, then add all ingredients except chopped onions and grated cheese.

Put lid on pot and reduce to a simmer. Cook for 4 hours.

Garnish with chopped onions and add grated cheese.

A good accompanyment for this chili is corn bread.

BEAUTIFUL STONE SHEEP GETS ME HALFWAY THROUGH GRAND SLAM

After the Dall Sheep hunt, I realized just how daunting sheep hunting is, so I made up my mind to train harder and get into better shape. I filled my backpack with 50-pound barbells and hiked up and down sand mounds at a small quarry at least twice a week for 12 weeks to get my legs in shape. I also walked two miles every day. After six weeks, I decided I was in great shape for a Stone Sheep hunt.

I'd set my sights on British Columbia and Scope Lake Outfitters for this hunt. After I spoke with Mr. Hansen, the owner of Scope Lake Outfitters, I was off and running. He addressed all of my concerns and gave me great solutions to the problems I'd identified.

✦   ✦   ✦

My son and my good friend Jimmy were coming with me on this trip. We flew from New York to the Yukon, which was a long trip. Once we got there, we boarded a floatplane and flew for another hour and a half to Scope Lake. The camp was beautiful, with small cabins surrounding the main cabin, all situated on the gorgeous lake.

The next morning, we boarded another floatplane and took a 45-minute flight to our next camp. The small cabin there would be our home for the next 10 days.

When Scott and I settled into our cabin, I was amazed to see so many famous names etched on the walls and beams. They included Jack O'Connor, world renowned outdoor writer, and my good friend, Johnny Rodriguez. Johnny had harvested more than three grand slams and taught me a lot about sheep hunting.

We ate our dinner, then sat around the campfire listening to stories about Scope Lake and some of the great sportsmen and women who had stayed at this camp.

Day one dawned and we were greeted with a splendid sun-drenched morning. Scott and I saddled up our horses and rode through the tall timber. We ventured into different crayons, and crossed rivers and streams.

Eventually, we came into an area hunters call Valley of the Rams. We saw a mountainside that was literally covered with sheep. We glassed 40 or so ewes and six rams, but unfortunately none of them were what I was hoping for.

Not a cloud floated in the sky that day, so we rode on to the next drainage basin. That's when the unforeseen happened. My guide's horse stepped on a yellow jacket nest. When this happend, his horse threw him, and he landed on his back. Thank God he was wearing a backpack to cushion his fall!

The horse darted off, and I dismounted and ran over to assist my guide as he lay on the ground. The fall had knocked the wind out of him, but he was okay. Once he could speak, he asked me to find his horse.

I agreed to try, but was skepitacal. I wasn't familiar with the territory and worried I might get lost. So, I decided I'd rely on my years of hunting experience to guide me and took note of the position of the sun and mountains before I left.

I rode for 30 minutes and finally found the horse at the bottom of a drainage basin grazing like nothing had happened. I approached quietly, grabbed his his bridle, and rode back to where I'd started.

We rested there for a short time and then headed back to camp. After this mishap, Scott and I were acutely aware of our surroundings. I cooked dinner, and let the guide rest.

The next morning, Scott, my guide, and I covered three miles that required crossing two streams. We headed into a valley shrouded in fog, and set up at the bottom to wait for the fog to clear so we could glass both sides of the valley.

I spotted three rams at the top of the valley, so we put together our game plan. We tied the horses and climbed, using every bit of cover we could find. We were at this for two hours.

Finally, we stopped 600 yards away from the sheep, so we could check them out. Only one of the three was legal. I elected to turn him down. He wasn't quite what I was looking for.

I was disappointed, so I was glad the climb down was extra easy. We did see four ewes on the way down, though.

We returned to our horses and moved into a different area. We glassed for an hour but didn't see any legal rams, so we headed back to camp.

Day three was like many others I've experienced while hunting. We ate an early breakfast, loaded up the horses, and rode for a good long while to a brand-new area. We schlepped along for four hours and found a spot between two mountains where we dismounted. We hobbled the horses and broke out our backpacks. We would walk up the riverbed. It was dry, indicating there hadn't been much rain during the season.

We found a high spot to do some glassing, and spotted two rams on the other side of the mountain. We decided to pack up right away and go after them.

So, back to the horses we went, then ended up riding for two hours before we got to the opposite side. We stalked the sheep up a drainage basin, then went after them on foot again.

We climbed for over an hour, ascending at a fast walk. Our goal to was to reach a large boulder sticking out of the side of the mountain. When we got there, we glassed to make sure the sheep were still grazing.

I used my rangefinder to range the two sheep at 900 yards. We slowed our stalk so we didn't start a shale slide — there was a lot of loose rock in this area. We closed the distance from 900 yards to 500, and set up there.

The sheep started grazing and were coming toward us. They had no idea we were there. As they kept moving, they ended up moving above us. We waited for two hours and they only moved another 50 yards.

At 450 yards, I decided it was now or never. I was using my trusty Winchester 7mm, as I do on all my sheep hunts. I perched it on my backpack and prepared for the shot. I checked my rangefinder one last time, because I knew I wasn't going to get a second chance.

One of the sheep was 425 yards away, the other was a bit farther, so deciding which to take was easy. Luckily, he was also the bigger of the two. I positioned my crosshairs on the sheep's shoulder. I knew if I could punch through his shoulders he wouldn't be able to run too far. I squeezed the trigger and thought I'd hit just where I'd planned.

Me with my full-curl stone sheep.

He ran uphill, and I realized my shot wasn't quite where I'd intended. I chambered another round and ranged the sheep at 650 yards. This was a Hail Mary shot. I hit him again, and he rolled down the shale for 75 yards and came to rest on a rock.

Even as tired as I felt, I found the energy to run uphill to reach the spot where he'd come to rest. My stone sheep was a legal, full-curl sheep. He was even a bit bigger than I'd thought when I spotted him.

I was so happy. No words could explain how I felt after the agonizing hours of training resulting in holding that sheep in my hands.

We caped out my prize and loaded it on our horses to return to camp. With this harvest, I'd made the halfway point in my quest to hunt the grand slam of North American wild sheep.

Oven Braised Stone Sheep Shanks

3 tablespoons olive oil, divided
1 tablespoon butter
1 large onion, coarsely chopped
1 rib of celery, coarsely chopped
1 medium carrot, coarsely chopped
4 cloves garlic, sliced

4 stone sheep shanks
1 dash salt and freshly ground black pepper
1 cup dry red wine
3 tablespoons tomato paste
2 cups chicken broth
1 cup beef broth
1/4 cup cider vinegar
4 sprigs fresh thyme
1 bay leaf

Heat the oven to 325° F.

In a large skillet or Dutch oven, heat 1 tablespoon of olive oil with butter. Add chopped onion, celery, and carrot. Cook, stirring until onion is softened. Add garlic and cook, stirring, for 2 minutes more. Remove to a large roasting pan, or Dutch oven.

Add rest of olive oil skillet. Sprinkle the sheep shanks with salt and pepper; saute over medium heat for about 8 minutes, turning to sear all sides. Add to chopped vegetables.

Deglaze skillet with the red wine. Simmer for 2 minutes. Add tomato paste, chicken broth, beef broth, and vinegar. Bring to a boil. Reduce heat and simmer 5 minutes. Pour over sheep shanks and add fresh thyme and bay leaf.

Cover pan tightly and bake for 1-1/2 hours. Remove lid and continue baking for 2 to 2-1/2 hours, turning the shanks occasionally. Meat should be very tender when done.

Rosemary Irish Stone Sheep

1 tablespoon olive oil
1 large onion, chopped
1-1/2 pounds sheep
    shoulder, sliced into
    quarters
salt

pepper
1 can beef broth
2 cups water
1/2 teaspoon dried thyme
3 sprigs rosemary

Pre-heat oven to 375° F.

Heat oil in a skillet over medium high heat, sauté onions until golden, then place in a 2-1/2 quart baking dish.

Salt and pepper sheep, and in the same skillet brown both sides of the meat, then put on top of onions in dish.

Pour beef broth and water over meat and onions, add seasonings, cover with tin foil and braise for 1 hour. Remove foil and continue to braise for another hour.

Serve with juices from dish

THE END OF MY 14-YEAR WAIT FOR A BIGHORN SHEEP

It's funny how my dreams and desires motivate me. I'd just harvested a Dall and Stone sheep, and I now planned to hunt the third sheep on my way to completing the Grand Slam.

At this point, I'd been applying in the State of Wyoming for 12 years, and hoped I'd get drawn soon for a Bighorn sheep. After all those years, I was beginning to think the day would never come. Finally, in the 14th year of my crusade, a letter from the Wyoming Fish and Game office arrived containing my bighorn sheep permit. I was in shock.

I immediately started researching the hunt, and decided on Fritz Meyer as my outfitter. He'd been in the sheep hunting business for 30 years and had a great reputation. I called him, and we hit it off immediately. I was relieved when my plans were finalized for the fall.

Before I knew it, I was on a plane headed to Casper, Wyoming. I spent the night at Fritz's home and his wife made a great dinner to fuel us before be began the hunt the next day.

The next morning, we loaded seven horses and enough food and gear for a 10-day hunt onto the trailers. We could oly access my chosen area by horseback. This was going to be an interesting hunt.

We got to the trail at 9 a.m., loaded up the horses and started my Bighorn sheep adventure. We stopped for lunch in view of the stunning mountains, and could hear a bull elk bugling. Shortly after that, an unbelievable royal elk (designated royal because it has 12 antler points) ventured out into a clearing right in front of us. I took this as a good sign for my impending hunt.

After lunch, we were back in the saddle, headed to the location where we'd pitch our tent camp. By the time we got there, we only had enough daylight left to setup the tents and have dinner.

When darkness fell, the stars looked so close it I felt like I could reach up and touch them. The air was crisp, dry and sweet-smelling. I got the feeling this might be as close to heaven as I'd get while still here on earth.

The sun shone bright in the powder blue sky the next morning as we glassed, looking for bighorn. We saw no sheep, but there sure was some beautiful scenery to enjoy as we rode at 8,000 feet above sea level.

As the day wound down, we made our way back to camp and had a quick dinner. My unproductive day was made worse by the fact that I felt a cold coming on.

The next morning, I felt like crap but knew I had to soldier on — I'd been waiting 14 years for this chance and a cold wasn't going to rob me of it. I swallowed some Advil, drank a bottle of water and got ready to face the day.

Can-do attitude only got me so far, and by mid-day I was undeniably sick. Fritz suggested we go back to camp, so I could rest, while he did some glassing.

I slept for two hours, and woke up thinking I heard a horse. I flipped open the tent flap but didn't see anyone. Instead, I had an uninvited guest — a huge grizzly bear.

I scrabbled around, trying to find my rifle shells. I wasn't going to take any chances because grizzly bear behavior can be unpredictable.

The closer he got to the camp, the more concerned I became. I didn't want to shoot him and, thankfully, I didn't have to. He finally decided the camp wasn't interesting and headed back into the woods.

When Fritz returned to camp, I told him about the unexpected guest. He said he'd also seen the bear a couple of times, but it only seemed curious.

Fritz said he'd found a possible ram for me. So, even though I felt terrible, I wanted to check it out the next day. I was not about to concede defeat to the common cold.

✦ ✦ ✦

I didn't sleep well that night. I even kept Fritz awake with my coughing.

The next morning, like a good soldier, I was up and ready at first light. We rode for two hours, and stumbled upon a legal, half-curl ram by mid-morning. I lined up my shot, pulled the trigger and missed. This was a first for me.

The ram was gone in a flash, and I felt sick, both literally and physically. By this point, I had a fever and the chills. It's no wonder I missed my shot.

Fritz told me I was in no shape to continue hunting, and we headed back to camp so I could rest and try to shake my illness. On the way, we glimpsed a ram lying on a stone ledge that jutted from a hillside. This guy was more than legal — he had a three-quarter curl.

Even feeling as bad as I did, I gave the sheep the once-over and decided to stalk him. I got within 200 yards of him, focused my scope and squeezed off the shot. He dropped right where he stood. I had my bighorn!

We returned to camp and closed it down. My sheep was harvested, and everyone else had already left. After that, we loaded our horses and headed to the truck. By the time we got back, I had a fever of 101.

Me and my Bighorn sheep — number three in my grand slam.

I rested for the next two days. When I felt better, I headed to Wyoming Fish and Game to have my sheep recorded aged and plugged. (Plugging is when a conservation officer drills a hole in a sheep's horns and inserts a numbered steel plug. The number is a reference to your name as the successful hunter.)

Although sheep hunting is physically demanding, it is also one of the most rewarding things I've ever done. I was now three sheep into completing the grand slam of sheep hunting!

Grilled Bighorn Backstrap

1 Bighorn backstrap loin, approximately 12 inches long
2 cloves garlic, minced

3 tablespoons butter
Dash lemon pepper
Dash of rubbed sage
1/2 cup butter, melted

Clean backstrap thoroughly, and trim all excess fat and muscle sheath. Rub lemon pepper and sage on backstrap and place in 13x9-inch dish.

Brown minced garlic in 1 tablespoon of butter in skillet over low heat, then pour over backstrap.

Cover and refrigerate for several hours so meat absorbs seasonings.

Sear both sides of backstrap quickly on very hot grill or skillet to seal in juices, then brush on melted butter and cook to taste on cooler place on grill. Turn several times and baste often.

Meat should be served medium to rare. (The longer you cook, the dryer and tougher the meat will be).

Note: Steaks can be grilled faster, but be cautious about over-seasoning and overcooking. Bighorn sheep meat has a delicate flavor and can easily be overpowered by heavy seasoning.

Coors Bighorn Sheep Stew

Vegetable oil
2 lbs. rocky mountain bighorn sheep, cut into 1 1/2 inch cubes
Flour for dredging
2 small cloves garlic, minced
1 6-oz. can tomato paste
2-1/4 cups Coors beer
2 bay leaves
1 teaspoon salt
1 teaspoon beef bouillon granules
1-1/2 teaspoon freshly ground black pepper
1 teaspoon sugar
1/2 teaspoon dried thyme
3/4 teaspoon dried oregano
8 to 10 pearl onions, peeled
6 carrots, peeled and cut into chunks
6 stalks celery, cut into chunks
1/2 lb. mushrooms, halved
6 small potatoes, peeled and cut into chunks

Heat 1/4 inch of oil in large skillet until shimmering. Dredge meat in flour and brown in hot oil. Transfer to large kettle. Add remaining ingredients. Cook over low heat for 3 hours or until meat is tender.

Serves 6

GRAND SLAM COMPLETE WITH THE DESERT BIGHORN SHEEP

I only needed one more sheep to complete my Grand Slam, but the chances of that happening weren't great because I had to win a draw in one of the states that had Desert Bighorn sheep tags. I'd tried all the drawings over a 10-year period before this. Even though I was discouraged, I kept at it for an additional five years, still without success.

Then, I suddenly had a glimmer of hope when my friend Johnny Zenz told me Nevada planned to have an auction for a Governor's License. The winner of the auction would get a license that was good for hunting any part of the state at any time during the legal season.

I asked Johnny what he thought the winning bid might be. He decided the number would be heavily influenced by how many people were participating in the auction.

I really wanted that tag, but worried about what it would cost me. I'd participated in similar auctions in the past, and had seen bids go as high as $125,000. I certainly wasn't willing to spend that much. I had the option to bid over the phone through Johnny, and he wanted to know just how high I would go. As crazy as it sounds, I told him $30,000 to $35,000. I'd spent my whole life hunting sheep, and I figured my Grand Slam was worth the cost.

My phone rang at midnight on the night of the auction. Johnny was at there, ready to place my bid. By that time, I'd decided to forget about my bid of $35,000 and asked him to open with a bid of $10,000. The bidding soon jumped to $15,000 then $20,000 and quickly moved to $25,000. Obviously, someone else wanted this tag badly.

There was a break in bidding, to give the auctioneer a chance to breathe, but the frenzy began again as things started back up. I guy I was bidding against raised his bid to $30,000. I countered with $32,000, which he upped to $34,000. I took a deep breath and told Johnny to go to $35,000. I was outbid again, and it didn't look like my competitor was going to stop any time soon.

Johnny yelled at me before the gavel came down to shatter my dream, and this was the only time in my life I listened to him. I sent the bid soaring to $40,000. The other guy bid $45,000; I bid $48,000. After he bested me again, I took a wild chance and bid $52,000. The gavel pounded and I'd won! I was the proud owner of the Nevada Governor's Tag.

I'd worked hard all my life, and saved my money for something important. I had no regrets about the purchase of this tag.

The next morning, I didn't know whether to feel ecstatic or check myself into the funny farm. Johnny called me to see how I was, and I told him I was great but apprehensive about how much I paid. Then, in the next breath I said we should forget about about the cost and go hunting, damn it!

Planning this hunt seemed to move go in slow motion, but I knew I needed to have patience. One of my dreams was a bout to come true and I was leaving nothing to chance.

The hunt took place in the fall of 2002. I jetted off to Reno, Nevada and was greeted by a beautiful blue sky and a temperature of 65 degrees when I left the plane. My good friend of 35 years, John B, joined me on this trip as an observer. I viewed John as a kindred spirit who was always up for an adventure.

The country where the sheep camp was located was beautiful, but it took quite a while to get there from the airport. By the time we arrived at our destination, it was late. We ate dinner and enjoyed the nice weather before turning in early.

The following morning, we set out to an area where John Zenz had seen sheep the week before. We sighted a few ewes, but didn't see any rams. The weather was changing on us, with the temperature dropping nearly 20 degrees by mid-afternoon, so we decided to call it a day. By the time we got back to camp, the wind had picked up, too. We ate our dinner in our comfortable tent and turned in so we'd be fresh for another go in the morning.

I got the shock of my life when I woke up the next morning to two inches of snow on the ground. It hadn't snowed in Reno in years. I hadn't brought enough cold-weather clothes to deal with this kind of weather.

We dressed as warmly as possible and decided to try a different area than the previous day. We saw some sheep in this new area, but none of them were legal.

That's the way it goes sometimes. No matter how hard you look, you don't find sheep. Then, the next day there are sheep are all over the place.

We covered every rock and every canyon that day but there just weren't any sheep anywhere. So, we split up to cover two ridges. I climbed to a high point and glassed for a while. I spotted two rams but no shooters.

After the long day, we returned to camp, praying that day three would be more eventful.

✦ ✦ ✦

The day dawned sunny, beautiful and cold. The snow still blanketed the ground and frosted the hills.

Johnny Zenz didn't think there were sheep in the area where we started that morning, but as soon as he voiced that opinion, I spotted a sheep clamboring up a rise. I jogged to the top of the rise to see if I could get a better look.

There was a beautiful Desert Bighorn sheep standing only 200 yards away. This was a chip shot. He stood broadside on a beautiful outcropping of rock, looking so regal against the snow.

Before Johnny Zenz could say a word or heft his binoculars to look at the ram, I dropped to my knee and checked him out with my scope. I learned a long time ago not to waste time looking through binoculars. I didn't want my sheep to have a chance to get away.

I clicked off the safety and squeezed the trigger on my rifle without haste. As the shot rang out, I realized my dream was complete. I'd just harvested my fourth sheep and achieved my North American Wild Sheep Grand Slam!

I found out I was the 1,049th person to ever accomplished this feat when I recorded my sheep with the North American Wild Sheep Foundation. It was an honor for me to be included with all other hunters who'd received this designation.

✦ ✦ ✦

When I got home from the hunt, my friends congratulated me and thought I'd announce the the end of my hunting career. That didn't happen because I knew in my heart that my escapades were far from over.

THIS IS TO CERTIFY THAT
John McAteer

has documented with

GSC OVIS

the successful taking of the four species of North American wild sheep, and has been

1046

in recognition of the

Grand Slam

YEAR COMPLETED

2002

Dennis

GSCO Executi

The Desert Bighorn sheep that completed my Grand Slam.

Juniperberry Rubbed Desert Bighorn Backstraps

1-2 lbs. strips of boneless Bighorn Loin (properly dry aged at least 2 weeks)
3-4 tablespoons olive oil

2 tablespoons fresh minced garlic
3-4 tablespoons Rub
Kosher or Sea Salt to taste

Rub:
2 teaspoons juniper berries
1 teaspoon black peppercorns
1/2 teaspoon kosher salt
1/2 teaspoon crushed red pepper

1 bay leaf
2 tablespoons extra-virgin olive oil
6 minced sage leaves
1 minced garlic clove

Trim all the silver skin from the loin. Brush with olive oil, and rub the meat with the garlic, then massage the meat with the rub. For the best results place in a zip lock bag overnight to allow the seasonings to penetrate.

Cook either over a very hot grill OR quick sear in an iron skillet. Quickly sear and cook evenly on all sides until rare (125° F internal temperature).

Allow the meat to rest to redistribute the moisture and let the residual heat finish the meat to a juicy medium rare.

BATTLING HIGH ALTITUTES FOR A TIBETEN BLUE SHEEP

Since I'd completed my Grand Slam, it was time to move forward to my next hunting adventure. After days of deliberation, I decided to hunt the Tibetan blue sheep. This promised to be a great challenge for this 60-year-old hunter.

Though all hunts have their challenges, the the 15,000–17,000 altitude for this trip would be a big one for me. I discovered there really is no training for hunting at high altitude, so I'd just have to hope I was in good enough shape to complete the task I'd set for myself.

I talked to hunting colleague Dennis Cambell, who'd just been on a successful Tibetan sheep hunt, about my concerns. He recommend I get a physical before attempting the hunt. I thought this was good advice, so I talked to my doctor, who was also a hunter. He gave me a clean bill of health but suggested I start taking a drug called Diamox six weeks before the trip. This medication thins the blood, allows for better circulation and combats altitude sickness.

For this epic adventure I traveled from New York to California, then to Beijing, China. While in Beijing, John B. and I visited the Great Wall of China. The story of its construction was mind-boggling. We also visited the Emperor's Palace and a Ming vase factory. I was amazed by the work and time involved to make these masterpieces.

After spending three days in Beijing, it was time to board another flight to Dulan, in the Chenzo Province. From there, we drove 14 hours to where we would start our hunt in the mountains of Tibet.

A medical advisor greeted us when we finally arrived at the tent camp, and made sure we were fit to start the hunt. The camp was well staffed, even providing workers to make sure the coal stoves in our yurts were kept stoked.

The thin air made breathing difficult, even without exerting myself. I was glad our climb would be done in increments. Base camp #1 was at 12,000 feet. We spent the night there and then moved on to the next camp at 14,000 feet. Finally, on the third day we arrived at the main camp, located at 15,000 feet. We stayed in this camp for the next two days so we could adapt to the altitude. All four of us could definitely feel the difference in altitude.

At the end of the second day, John, Pat, Bill, and I took the time to visit a Tibetan monastery to see the monks during their prayer vigil. The silence was mesmerizing. We were given the opportunity to taste some Mongolian cuisine and also had the privilege of calling upon a holy man at his home. He invited us to sit in a circle and then passed around a goblet that contained something similar to moonshine. That stuff could peel paint off a car!

Our host instructed us to dip our fingers into the goblet, make a silent wish, drink from the goblet, and then pass it to the next person. All was going well until I saw one of the Mongolians pick his noise before dipping his finger. That put an end to my drinking for the evening.

The next morning Ming, my interpreter and guide, suggested we take a drive to see some of the surrounding area. All four of us hunters piled into the camp truck and Ming drove us onto a frozen stream that would apparently act as our road. This made me extremely uncomfortable because I was afraid the truck would break through the ice and we'd get stuck.

As our joyride down the stream continued, we finally steered onto terra firma. We then turned around and followed the stream back to camp.

The nights here were so cold that the staff checked on each of us in our tents every two hours. While they were there, they'd stoke the stove, which sat in the center. At approximately 6 a.m. every morning, a medical technician would come in to take our blood pressure and our temperatures.

On my first morning there, the technician handed me a thermometer. I assumed that I knew how to use a thermometer, so I placed it under my tongue. The technician chuckled, and I was horrified when I learned that the thermometer had been in the armpit of everyone else in camp. I'd learned my lesson. Next time, I'd be more patient and wait to receive instructions before assuming I knew what to do.

That night, Ming said the cook was planning a special chicken dinner for me. I must admit I was hungry because up to that point I'd been surviving on black coffee and noodles.

We went to the mess tent and sat around a humungous round table. We had an interpreter — none of us spoke Mongolian, and none of them spoke English. The camp cook banged two big pots down on the table. As he took the lids off the pots, I could clearly see we were indeed having chicken, but they were completely intact, including gizzards, heads, and feet.

My appetite vanished. This was the first and only hunt I'd been on where the food was horrible. So, I continued with my diet of black coffee and noodles.

After the disappointing dinner, we called it a night because we had an early start in the morning.

✦　✦　✦

Three guides arrived at my yurt with Tibetan ponies first thing the next morning. The ponies seemed tiny compared to what I was used to, and I couldn't imaging riding them up the mountain. I was sure my feet would hit the ground when I mounted, but all was good so I slung my rifle over my shoulder and resigned myself to the miniature pony ride.

The temperature hovered at 15 degrees, and the stamina of my pony amazed me. He tackled the rocky mountain terrain easily and carefully avoided the icey rocks. As we approached a small slope, for some reason my pony decided to abruptly put on the brakes and toss me over his head. My feet caught in the stirrups and kept me from taking a header. I was lucky I didn't get hurt and the horse didn't move an inch until my guide could pry my feet out of the stirrups and get me back into hunting mode.

After that, our party climbed an additional 1,500 to 1,800 feet higher than base camp. Breathing was really a chore at this point.

We spied some blue sheep on the side of the mountain, so my guide and I stopped the ponies and broke out our spotting scopes. As I looked the sheep over, my guide tried to get me to shoot one of them. I used hand gestures to let him know the sheep wassn't what I was looking for.

We moved on to the next range of mountains, and as we entered the valley we observed a band of blue sheep grazing. Some of them were even bedded down. We glassed the

45 or so animals, and I didn't immediately see any I considered worthy.

But, as I kept looking, I saw a ram bedded down behind a boulder. He looked promising, but I wanted to be sure. After looking more closely, I saw that he had a large set of horns. So, I spent 30 minutes stalking him.

I got to within 450 yards of him, but could go no further because I ran out of cover. Up close, I could see he was a fine specimen and I resolved he would be mine.

I completed my set up, using a pair of bipods on my rifle so my shot would be steady. I wanted to wait for the ram to stand so I could take a broadside shot. I waited for 45 minutes in the 15-degree weather. Finally, he got up.

I had a perfect broadside shot. I positioned my crosshairs two inches above his back. I was using a 7mm mag with a 160-grain Nosler petition bullet. I steadied myself and prepared for a long shot. I squeezed the trigger, and the bullet found its mark. The ram dropped less than three feet from where it was shot.

Sheep number six was now in the books for me. It took me 45 minutes to walk the 400 yards up the mountain. It was a phenomenal chore at that altitude. I was elated and exhausted as I reached my Tibetan blue sheep. I sat down to catch my breath and realized that he was a lot bigger than I'd thought, which made it even better.

Being able to hunt in the great country of China, as well as meet new people and see their cultures was as exciting

High in the mountains with my Tibetan Blue sheep.

for me and just as the memorable as the hunt. This outing proved to me that you never know what you're capable of until you push yourself.

Tibetan Blue Sheep and Rice Pilaf

2 cups basmati rice
4 heads garlic, whole
1/2 cup vegetable oil
2 pounds boneless leg of
　　sheep, cut into 3-inch
　　pieces
2 large onions, thinly sliced
2 tablespoons cumin seed

2 tablespoons coriander seed
1/2 cup fresh barberries or
　　chopped sour cherries
1 teaspoon whole black
　　peppercorns
2 cups boiling water to cover
2 tablespoons salt

Place basmati rice in a large bowl and cover with warm water. Set aside. Wash heads of garlic. Set aside.

Heat oil in a dutch oven or large skillet over high heat until smoking, then add meat, turning occasionally until it is evenly browned, about 10 minutes. Stir in the onions; cook and stir until the onion has softened and browned, about 10 minutes.

Stir in the carrots; cook and stir until they have softened, about 10 minutes. Sprinkle with cumin, coriander, barberries/cherries, and peppercorns. Drop whole garlic heads into the mixture, stirring to distribute ingredients.

Reduce heat to medium. Cover and cook for 30 minutes.

Drain rice then wash with hot water. Pour cleaned rice over the sheep mixture in an even layer. Slowly pour in the boiling water. The rice should be covered with about 3/4 inch of water. Do not stir. Season with salt, and reduce heat to medium-low. Cover and cook until rice is tender, about 20 minutes. Stir rice and lamb together, and serve with the garlic heads on top.

THE OUTHOUSE GRIZZLY BEAR

I had just booked an archery Stone Sheep hunt in northern British Columbia and was super excited to be hunting with one of the most famous guides in the world, Bill Love of Love Bros. & Lee Outfitters. For those of you who don't recognize the name, Bill Love was the late Fred Bear's number one choice as a guide when hunting in British Columbia. It was an honor to get to spend time with and hunt grizzly bear with this great man.

After a scenic flight, the floatplane set down on a beautiful lake and I was greeted by a true mountain man, 77-year-old Mr. Bill Love, when I stepped off the floatplane.

As soon as I got my gear stowed, we strapped on our backpacks and headed off to sheep country. We'd been at it for about seven hours when we crested the top of the mountain and were met by a breathtaking view. A short time later, we arrived at the small cabin where we'd be staying. It contained only two beds and a small cook stove. .

As you might imagine, this mountaintop cabin did not have running water, so Bill grabbed a pail and hiked down to a nearby stream for some ice-cold, crystal-clear mountain water that had been purified my Mother Earth herself. Now, that's something you won't find in the city!

Bill made us some Kool-Aid, and as daylight faded we sat there sipping our drinks. I wasn't a huge fan, so Bill offered me a glass of cold water instead and told me to go outside, dig a hole, and bury the Kool-Aid.

We ate a quick dinner and went off to bed for a good night's rest. That fresh mountain air knocked me right out.

Following one of the best nights of sleep I'd ever had, I woke the next morning and enjoyed a cup of coffee, made with invigorating mountain water.

As usual after a cup of coffee, things moved right along, if you know what I mean. Bill directed me to the place where I could take care of business, and I drifted down the path through the pines to a small clearing in the trees.

I soon recognized the correct spot when I saw two branches cut from a pine tree positioned between two gigantic trees. Another broken branch held a roll of toilet paper.

As I sat on the Rocky Mountain toilet and prepared for my morning deposit, I heard a loud crash. I peered through the pines and saw a grizzly bear that must've weighed 600 pounds sitting only 20 yards from me. It was digging in the exact place where I'd buried my raspberry Kool-Aid the night before.

I froze and wondered if I was going to be his next snack. By now, those two sticks were causing me a ton of discomfort, but I sure wasn't going to move a muscle. I didn't feel the urge to make that deposit anymore, either.

The bear was growling up a storm and dirt was flying as he looked for a treat he wasn't going to find. I remained still, like a statue, for more than 30 minutes as that grizzly dug a hole several feet wide and a couple of feet deep.

Bill started to worry when I'd been gone for more than 30 minutes, so he looked out the cabin door and saw the grizzly bear digging right next to me. His 30/30 caliber rifle rested just inside the door, and without hesitation he chambered a cartridge and fired into the sky. When the bear didn't move, he chambered and fired another round. That finally convinced the bear to move along.

You can't imagine how relieved I was when I heard those shots! My posterior was screaming at this point and I was happy to be able to move again.

When I got back to the cabin, Bill laughed and said I'd been held hostage by the bear for nearly 50 minutes.

The moral of this story is, don't bury your raspberry Kool-Aid anywhere near the outhouse!

OUTFITTERS AND GUIDES

This list of fine people and businesses were instrumental in helping me reach my goals:

Guided Artic Expedition

Scope Lake Outfitters: Darwin & Wendy Cary, 5615 Deadpine Drive, Kelowna, B.C., V1P 1A3 Canada. Website: www.scooplake.com

Jerry Boren, deceased

John Bosco, deceased

Johnny Rodriguez, deceased

Tommy Teits

Love Brothers and Lee: Ron Fleming, Guide & Outfitter. Love Bros & Lee, 1857 Kispiox Valley Rd., Hazelton, B.C., Canada V0J 1Y5. Website: lovebroslee.com

Bill Love, Master Guide

John Zenzs

Alex Letendar

Steve Jones

Jack Humes Adventures: 86 Chemin Robinson, Wentworth, QC J8H 0G3, Canada, Phone: +1 450-533-5999

Tri T Outfitters

Jeff Jandreau

Jerry Matthews

Dale Boyer

Squaw Lake Outfitter: Phone: 819-483-1514, email: info@squawlake.com, website: www.squawlake.com

Nictau Lodge: 4020 Route 385, Nictau, New Brunswick Canada E7G 3B2. Phone: 1-506-356-8014, mail: NictauLodge@hotmail.com, website: www.nictaulodge.com

Gabe Delagza

Caesar's Lodge

Benny Brasard

Little River Plantation: 1314 Warwick Hwy, Ashburn, GA 31714. Phone: (229) 567-3584, website: www.littleriverga.com

Big Rack Adventure Safari Klindberg World Wide Travel

Mayfield Ranch: Josh Boness, Manager. PO Box 3889, San Angelo, TX 76902. Phone: 325.656.1213, email: josh@mayfieldranch.com, website: www.mayfieldranch.com

Mel Gillis

Phil Gay

Jerry Ippolito

Pope and Young Club: Box 548, Chatfield, MN 55923. Phone: 507-867-4144, email: admin@pope-young.org, website: pope-young.org

Legends of the Outdoors: Garry Mason, 11020 Hwy. 69S, Springville, TN 38256-5414. Phone: 731-593-0171, email: grmason@bellsouth.net, website: www.legendsoftheoutdoors.com

Safari Club International: Website: www.safariclub.org Phone: (520) 620-1220.

National Wild Turkey Foundation: 1-800-THE-NWTF (843-6983) Email: membership@nwtf.net, website: ww.nwtf.org/

Bob Foulkrod

For more information about anyone on this list, please email me at jmmo45o@aol.com

From left to right are Dale Boyer, CEO Bad Bear Productions; John McAteer, 2018 Legends of Outdoors National Hall of Fame Inductee; and Garry Mason, Founder and CEO Legends of the Outdoors National Hall of Fame.

2018 HALL OF FAME HONOR BESTOWED

In May of 2018, I heard from Garry Mason, founder and CEO of the Legends of the Outdoors National Hall of Fame. He was calling to notify me that I, John McAteer, the boy who grew up in the Bronx, was going to be inducted into his company's hall of fame.

This was one of the greatest surprises I've ever experienced. So, on August 25, 2018, surrounded by family and friends in Nashville, Tennessee, I accepted the award. I got to share this moment with both past and present inductees.

Left, me holding the plaque I was awarded. Above, the belt buckle given to me by Bob Foulrod. I cherish it.

It was a wonderful way to commemorate my hunting journey, and I received the honor with a sense of great pride.

I've always strived to be the best I can be, whether it was raising my family, my career or reaching goals I set for myself. This award acknowledged all the work and effort I've put into my hunting over the years, and I'm humbled to join the ranks of the other great hunters who've received this honor before me.

With Charlton Heston, receiving Leather Stocking Award From National Rifle Association.

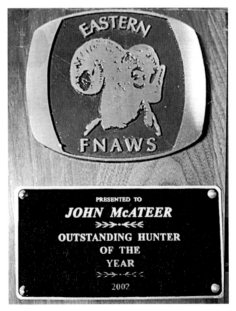

John received the Eastern Chapter Wild Sheep Foundation Hunter of the Year award in 2002.

WRAPPING IT UP

Life is a journey with many twists and turns. For me, they came in the form of mountains, rivers and streams. I've had the pleasure of living many rewarding and truly fascinating moments in the great outdoors, and I am blessed to be able to work outside and deal with the natural world.

I have enjoyed hunting and fishing all over the world and have met so many great people who have shared their amazing stories with me. This experience has made me realize that my journey has yet to come to an end. It's in my nature to continue to look for the next great adventure, and that's just what I'll do — though I might have to slow things down a bit.

Something my dad always said has become my mantra: "Expect the worst and hope for the best because failure is not an option, it's merely the steppingstone on the way to success."

To you, dear reader, I say, "Find your passion. Do the things you truly love and let that guide you to happiness. Never fear the unknown, as darkness will always give way to the light of another day."

Hunt hard and hunt safe, my friends.

John Mc Ateer